OVER THE SEA TO SKYE

Br

Frontispiece: PRINCE CHARLES WEARING THE JACOBITE
EMBLEM IN THE FORM OF A WHITE KNOTTED RIBBON.

OVER THE SEA TO SKYE

THE FORTY-FIVE

BY

JOHN SELBY

HAMISH HAMILTON
LONDON

First published in Great Britain, 1973
by Hamish Hamilton Ltd
90 Great Russell Street London WC1
Copyright © 1973 by John Selby

SBN 241 02203 7

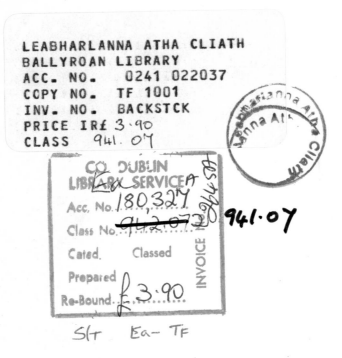

Filmset and printed by BAS Printers Limited,
Wallop, Hampshire

CONTENTS

ACKNOWLEDGEMENTS

I am indebted to the Duke of Atholl for allowing me to use photographs of pictures at Castle Blair, also to Mrs. Marr of the West Highland Museum, Fort William for allowing photographs to be taken for me of the exhibits in her care, also to the Staff of the Scottish National Portrait Gallery and the Scottish United Services Museum for assistance with the illustrations. I wish to thank Mr. D. W. King and the Staff of the Ministry of Defence Library (Central and Army) for their help, also Lieutenant-Colonel G. A. Shepperd and the Staff of the Library of the Royal Military Academy, Sandhurst. I am indebted for their help and encouragement to Mrs. Jean Notcutt of Edinburgh, Colonel Robin Maclagan of Fort George, Miss Myrtle Maclagan, Miss Helen Orchard, Mrs. Betty Robertson and Mrs. Alison Mackenzie. I wish to thank my publisher Mr. Christopher Sinclair-Stevenson of Hamish Hamilton Ltd. for his immense help. Finally, I want to thank Mrs. Kathleen Longstaff for typing the manuscript with such care.

LIST OF ILLUSTRATIONS

Colour

Black and white

Maps drawn by Patrick Leeson

Chapter I

FONTENOY 1745

*'It is not easy to form an opinion as to whether the result
will prove good or bad for my affairs.'*
PRINCE CHARLES EDWARD

Shortly after the Battle of Fontenoy, news reached the leader of the
Allied army in Flanders that his cousin Charles Edward had set sail for
Scotland. But William, Duke of Cumberland was not unduly concerned,
for there had been similar alarms in 1743 and 1744 and nothing had
come of them.

All his life Prince William had loved soldiers and soldiering. From the
age of five, he was regularly drilling a company of boys outside his
nursery window, in the manner of his grandfather's guards. When he
was nineteen he spent a year or so at sea, but returned to his first passion
the army; and in 1743 accompanied George II to command a division
in the War of the Austrian Succession, fighting bravely at his father's
side at Dettingen. When his horse carried him into the midst of the
enemy, he was shot in the calf by mistake by one of his own men; but he
refused to have his wound dressed until a badly wounded French officer
lying near had been attended to: 'Begin with the French officer,' he said;
'he is more badly wounded than I am.' The Prince's conduct was
remarked on by James Wolfe who at only sixteen was precociously the
adjutant of his regiment: 'The Duke behaved as bravely as any man
could do. I had the honour of speaking to him just as the battle began,
and was myself often afraid of being dashed to pieces by the cannon-
balls, yet the Prince gave his orders with complete calmness.' Two
days after the battle George promoted his son lieutenant general as a
recognition of his services – a gesture which was generally welcomed –
and on 16 March, 1745, just before his twenty-fourth birthday, the Duke
was gazetted 'Captain General of all his Majesty's land forces employed
abroad with his Majesty's allies'. Again the advancement was popular,
for most people had confidence in the large, imperturbable young man
whom they had come to associate with victory.

Within a month of his new appointment, Cumberland had left to take
up his post. On arrival it was obvious that discipline needed tightening
up after a winter of inactivity, and he set to work to put the matter right.

Cumberland as a child watched his grandfather's guards at practice outside his nursery window. By Bernard Lens

George II by Shackleton

He gave his whole attention to the new command, and his massive scarlet-coated figure on his seventeen-hand Yorkshire hunter was seen daily around the encampments. Combining the authority of his station with the reputation he had won on the battlefield he was both admired and feared; but he was genuinely popular in spite of his high standards. His severity was indicated early on in an instruction to his officers to put duty before pleasure, and in an order to his men to observe strict discipline as he was determined to show no mercy to anyone who misbehaved. His care and attention, though, had effect, for his British and Hanoverian troops became a splendid body of men. In contrast, his Dutch allies who did not come so directly under his influence never reached the same standard.

In the spring of 1745 the French advanced into Flanders and laid siege to Tournai, and the Duke left Brussels and marched his men south to try to relieve the fortress. He went, however, by a circuitous route and this gave time to the French under the formidable Marshal de Saxe to move a large body of troops five miles east to Fontenoy where a strong defensive position was set up athwart the Allied route to Tournai.

The Allies reached the village of Vezon a mile or so east of the carefully prepared French position on 11 May. The main French strongpoints were the Redoubt d'Eu on the edge of Barry Wood in the north, the village of Fontenoy in the centre, and a line of redoubts running westward from Fontenoy to the town of Antoing by the River Scheldt in the rear. The Allied plan was for the Dutch and the small Austrian contingent to attack in the south between Fontenoy and Antoing while the British and Hanoverians passed through the gap between the Redoubt d'Eu and Fontenoy into the heart of the French position: towards, in fact, the vantage point by Notre Dame de Bois where Louis XV, the Dauphin and Marshal de Saxe were stationed.

When the British advance began, the strength of the flanks on either side of the gap soon became apparent, as fire from the Redoubt d'Eu and Fontenoy raked the column. Brigadier Ingoldsby was detached with a small force to deal with the Redoubt d'Eu; but mishandled the operation and achieved nothing. The bombardment of the British cavalry in the van was so severe that they were stopped in their tracks, and the infantry had to be moved up through their intervals to lead the advance instead. There was a ridge in front which hid the enemy from view, but when the British of the front line had topped this ridge, they suddenly saw the enemy close in front. They gave a cheer, to which the French replied in a similar manner. '*Tirez les premiers, Messieurs les Français,*' then called out the British commander; but the French leader replied, 'No, Gentlemen, we never shoot first.' These exchanges were not just medieval courtesies. Ever since the French Guards met with a reverse at the Battle of Lens in 1648, mainly because of opening fire too soon at too great a range and wasting their first volley, they had been ordered never to fire first. At Fontenoy, however, the leading troops were so close that it did not matter, for the British fired first yet fared well. They delivered a devastating volley, laying low 700 of the Gardes Françaises opposing them; then they moved forward, firing by battalions. The enemy cavalry hurled themselves on them only to stagger back broken; a French trooper said later, 'It was like charging flaming fortresses.' The French withered under the hail of lead, and nothing could withstand the British infantry as they marched steadily towards the French camp.

The British lines of red-coated infantry pressed on into the French position, gradually coalescing, as they passed through the narrowest part of the gap, into one huge column against which the Maison du Roi and one of the six Irish regiments in the French service threw themselves in vain. Meanwhile, the French gunners were in a frenzy, loading their pieces with stones when their grape-shot was expended. This was the moment of crisis for the French; but Marshal de Saxe did not lose his nerve. Although so dropsical that he had to be borne in a litter, he had retained his skill as a tactician. Seeing that the Dutch and Austrians were being held in the south, he committed all his reserves, consisting of the remaining Irish regiments, several line regiments, and the French and Swiss Guards, against Cumberland's great column. The Irish 'Wild Geese' charged, yelling, against the British right, the others assaulted their left; combined with the faltering fire from the French guns this was sufficient, first to halt the column and then to cause it to fall back. So, early in the afternoon, the Duke ordered his drummers to beat out the order to retreat. The retirement was performed in perfect order, the rearguard facing about at measured intervals and firing volleys to hold off the pursuers. The hard-fought encounter cost each side about 7,000 casualties, and in this respect they finished on equal terms; but, by remaining on the field while the Allies drew away, the French foiled the attempt to relieve Tournai and may be said to have won the battle.

At the end, Marshal de Saxe was helped on to his horse by his faithful guard of Saxon Uhlans and led to meet Louis XV. It was the first time since 1356 that a French King and his eldest son had fought side by side; but, unlike George II and Cumberland at Dettingen, they were observers rather than participants. At the moment of crisis, the Dauphin, who had already donned his cuirass, mounted his horse with the intention of following the veteran marshal to the front; but, on being requested to stay at the King's side, he remained at the vantage point of Notre Dame de Bois. When the massive British column first broke through towards the camp, the royal headquarters were thrown into alarm. The King's boots were even brought so that he could mount his horse and retire from the battlefield, but to his credit he did not do so. His presence helped sustain the fortitude of his troops, and that seems to have been his main contribution. He did not glory in a fight like his German cousins, quite the reverse. When night fell he led the Dauphin round the battlefield, and showing him the thousands of dead said, 'My son, look at this dreadful scene and never shed your subjects' blood in an unjust war.'

In spite of his defeat Cumberland was able to gain some comfort from the encounter. He had acquitted himself well against one of the greatest commanders of the age, and had gained valuable experience. Even Saxe admitted that it had been a near thing, and that his victory had depended on being able to commit all his reserves against the encroaching column. Had the Dutch attacked more vigorously in the south, thus requiring more troops to hold them, Saxe would have been unable to use his reserves in the north. As he said to Louis after the battle, 'You see, Sire, on what the fate of battles turns.' Frederick the Great of Prussia was even more generous in his praise of the attack by the Duke of Cumberland's column. 'A quarter-wheel to the right, or a quarter-wheel to the left, or even both at once,' he said, 'would have brought him victory.'

One advantage which Cumberland gained from the battle was the knowledge of how the Scots fought and this was to stand him in good stead later. The Royal Scots and the Black Watch both distinguished themselves. The Royal Scots had their origin as a force serving the French kings: but Louis XIV lent some of them to Charles II at the Restoration to form the nucleus of his standing army, and they were retained as the First Regiment of Foot in the British Army. They were in the front line at Fontenoy and fought like lions. The Black Watch were embodied as a regiment of 1,000 men in 1739. Drawn from General Wade's independent companies of loyal Highlanders[1], they became the Highland Regiment of Foot (43rd, later 42nd). Their Colonel was Lord John Murray, brother of James, Duke of Atholl, and the Jacobite Marquis of Tullibardine; at Fontenoy they fought under their Lieutenant-Colonel Sir Robert Munro. Early on they were diverted to attack a redoubt on the outskirts of Fontenoy and were more successful than Brigadier Ingoldsby's men had been against the Redoubt d'Eu to the north. According to Doddridge:[2] 'Finding the body of the French forces deeply entrenched behind the battery, they did not give over the charge, but bravely drew up to attack them. Sir Robert, according to the usage of his countrymen ordered the whole regiment to clap to the ground on receiving the French fire, and as soon as it was discharged to spring up and march close to the enemy, when they were to pour their fire upon them and then retreat, drawing up in order. This mode of attack they accordingly repeated several times, driving the French with

1. *Wade, besides building roads to move his men around easily, had reconstituted companies of loyal Highlanders to act as police, see Appendix 1.*
2. *Life of Colonel Gardiner.*

6

great slaughter on their own lines.' The French were not slow to acknowledge their fighting qualities. One wrote: 'The Highland furies rushed in upon us with more violence than ever did a sea driven by a tempest.' And then added, plaintively, 'We gained a victory, but may I never see such another.'

Cumberland was pleased with the way all his infantry had behaved during the advance through the gap, as well as with the manner in which they carried out the withdrawal; but he was especially impressed by the Black Watch's storming of the redoubt at Fontenoy village. Because of this, he said he would grant them any favour in his power. Their request was an unexpected one. According to the Regiment's historian Archibald Forbes, 'they asked him to pardon one of their comrades who had been tried by court-martial for allowing a prisoner to escape, and who was under sentence of heavy corporal punishment which might very easily kill him, and in any case would bring disgrace on the regiment. The favour was instantly granted!' Forbes continues, 'The nature of this

Lord John Murray who commanded the Black Watch, 43rd later 42nd of Foot. He was a brother of Duke James of Atholl, the Marquess of Tullibardine and Lord George Murray

request, the feeling that suggested it, and in short the general qualities of the corps, impressed his Royal Highness the more since at the time he had never been to Scotland, and had not had any means of studying the character of the Highland soldier.' At Fontenoy an individual Highlander with a broadsword had proved more than a match for a French infantryman with a bayonet. By the time his own men had to face Highlanders in the field the Duke had devised a drill to give the man with the bayonet the advantage. He ordered him where possible not to attack his own immediate adversary, but rather the Highlander advancing on his comrade on the right hand. He was also told to thrust with the bayonet under this clansman's sword arm, so that the latter could not use his targe in his left hand to protect himself.

Although Cumberland gained a personal reputation from the battle, its immediate effect for the Allies was unfortunate. Ten days afterwards, the Dutch surrendered the citadel of Tournai after a defence which added nothing to their laurels. The Allies were unable to protect both Ghent and Brussels and saw Ghent fall in July, followed by Bruges and Oudenarde. In August, Ostend and Nieuport surrendered, and in September, Ath. Then, as soon as news arrived confirming Charles Edward's landing in Scotland, all but a few of Cumberland's regiments were sent back home. Finally, the Duke went himself.

The 1745 uprising which brought back the Duke of Cumberland from Flanders had its beginnings in 1740 when nine prominent Jacobites met in Edinburgh and formed an association to take up arms for James 'the moment a sufficient number of French troops could be landed in Scotland'. Nothing much was attempted immediately, but by 1743 envoys employed by the Edinburgh Association were passing to and from James's headquarters in order to seek assistance from the French monarch and his ministers for new ventures. The reaction of Cardinal Fleury to these supplications was to promise French help directly it was clear that many prominent people in Britain were supporters of the Stuart cause. This placed the Jacobites in a difficult position: for the number of their supporters could not be reckoned without an uprising; and yet they had planned to take up arms only when French troops landed. Then Cardinal Fleury died, and renewed demands had to be made to his successors. Cardinal Tencin who replaced Cardinal Fleury as chief minister and Amelot de Chaillon the foreign minister were both favourably inclined to help James, if only because it was a way of striking at Britain; but to start with they were too preoccupied to give the matter much attention. Tencin gave the first Jacobite envoy two minutes of his time, and the French foreign minister only vaguely promised help 'when the situation of affairs would permit'. However, Tencin, who owed his cardinal's hat to James's recommendation, later became co-operative, with the result that expeditions were planned which included French support.

James remembering the disappointments of the 1708 and 1715 uprisings did not propose to take part: instead, he nominated his eldest son Prince Charles Edward to take his place. Charles had much less experience as a military commander than his father who had fought at Malplaquet; but he possessed compensatory qualities. Although slight of build, he was strong and active, and capable of making long marches without tiring. Also, to good looks and a dignified mien were added natural leadership qualities and charm, which James lacked. Charles's only appearance on a battlefield had been in 1734 when at the age of fourteen he was present under the Duke of Liria at the Italian town of Gaeta where the Spanish prince Don Carlos was besieging an Austrian force. There was little Prince Charles could do at Gaeta; but by standing in the trenches and showing he did not mind being shot at, he demonstrated that he was as brave as the rest of his family, and a true Stuart.

The Old Pretender, the father of Prince Charles, by Blanchet

He stayed on until the town surrendered, and towards the end, when the walls of a house he was in were being punctured by cannon-balls, staunchly refused to seek a safer spot. The result was that Liria was able to report to Charles's father that he had been brave and soldier-like while in his charge. There was talk of joining the Spanish army in Sicily; but it came to nothing, for James did not want to risk the life of his son and heir further. Other aspects of Prince Charles's education were a little more thorough than his military training. He appears to have made some progress at his books under his Irish tutor Sir Thomas

Charles at the age of fourteen. Studio of A. David

Sheridan[1], and he became an accomplished musician. The power of Charles's charm was demonstrated in 1737 when at the age of seventeen he made a most successful grand tour of the Italian city states, Venice, Padua, Palma and the rest. They vied with one another in showing hospitality, and this caused some displeasure to their accredited British envoys who considered too much attention was being paid to the son of the Pretender; but everyone agreed that the Prince's demeanour on the tour was beyond reproach.

An expedition with French support planned for 1743 was never carried out, but was replaced in 1744 by one in which Marshal de Saxe, with Charles and a force of 6,000, attempted an invasion of England from Dunkirk. In order to achieve surprise an elaborate arrangement was evolved to bring Charles secretly from Rome to Dunkirk. The Prince and his brother Henry set out on a boar hunt in Italy, and then Charles slipped off without telling anybody and took a circuitous route partly by land and partly by sea to the South of France. The ruse delayed the knowledge of his departure from Italy, but he was recognised by a British agent in France, and traced to Paris, and from there to Gravelines near Dunkirk. This combined with obvious warlike preparations going on at Dunkirk and the passage up the Channel of a French fleet from Brest warned the British that another invasion attempt was about to take place, and the necessary defensive preparations were set in motion.

However, more than any other factor it was the weather which caused the failure of the 1744 attempt. After the French fleet had put to sea from Dunkirk, a severe gale sprang up, and the storm not only sent the supporting French naval vessels back to the safety of Brest harbour, but also wrecked several transports so that many soldiers and sailors were drowned and a considerable quantity of warlike stores lost. The vessel carrying Prince Charles was one of those which managed to weather the storm and get back to Dunkirk; and from Dunkirk he returned to Gravelines to await the summons to join a new expedition which he confidently expected to be arranged soon. According to the French historian Tail-lander, who quotes a letter of the French foreign minister, the view was that as the value of surprise had been lost no further attempt should be made for the present. Certainly the letters that Saxe sent to Prince Charles do not indicate that he was averse to making another attempt, and it seems that it was vetoed by the King and his ministers in agreement with James. To the latter the failure of Saxe's expedition had been

1. *According to a tradition in the Sheridan family Sir Thomas was the son of a Protestant Irish officer, killed at the Battle of the Boyne, and Princess Hélène a daughter of James II and Anne Hyde before their marriage, and was thus a nephew of James III, Prince Charles's father. Charles became deeply attached to his indulgent tutor, and valued his advice.*

a cruel blow. Never of a very sanguine temperament he had for once been quite hopeful of the expedition from Dunkirk. It was said that he even ordered new liveries for his servants to wear as soon as he heard the news of Prince Charles entering London in triumph. Anyway, because of his disappointment he did not favour another attempt immediately.

For a time Charles waited at Gravelines hoping to hear that the French King had given orders to Saxe to make a new attempt. When he learnt that postponement was definite, he still did not despair. He sent a message to Earl Marischal, who had been in command of the ships in the 1719 uprising, to invite his assistance, and when Marischal refused, declared he would hire a fishing boat and sail alone to Scotland where he felt sure many would flock to his standard. Then he changed his mind and went to Paris where he took up his abode in the house of Aeneas Macdonald[1] a young banker. The two became great friends and for a few months enjoyed together the gay life of Paris and Versailles. At no time, however, was Prince Charles able to gain an audience of King Louis, and so was unable to make a personal supplication for renewed French help. In Aeneas Macdonald's house he was joined by his old tutor Sir Thomas Sheridan, and a clergyman George Kelly who acted as his secretary until replaced by Murray of Broughton. At this period there was a welcome improvement in Prince Charles's finances. He came to an agreement with his father's Paris bankers whereby loans were made not only to meet his creditors but also to provide 160,000 livres for future expenditure, and the King of France graciously doubled his allowance making it 3,000 livres a year.

In the early months of 1745 the campaign in Flanders began, and when the news of the French victory at Fontenoy was received, the Jacobites began to try to assess its value to their cause. In spite of the obvious result that the defeat of their men would make the British people dislike the French still more, and therefore perhaps those the French supported, most of the Jacobites considered that it brought advantages, as the attention of the British army was now fully occupied. Prince Charles, it seems, was less sure, for in writing to one of his father's agents who had sent him information about the battle he observed, 'It is not easy to form an opinion as to whether the result will prove good or bad for my affairs; but in any case I am determined to go to Scotland though unaccompanied even by a single company of soldiers.'

---

1. *Brother of Kinlochmoidart, whose Jacobite father had fought at Sheriffmuir in 1715.*

Chapter II

LOCH-NAN-UAMH

*'I have obtained the services of Antoine Walsh who un-
doubtedly knows his business perfectly well and is a good
seaman.'*

STUART PAPERS

Charles's determination to go to Scotland caused the French ministers
to become more favourable to the Jacobite cause, and although unwilling
to offer overt help, they instructed Lord Clare who was commander of
the Irish Brigade to organise what unofficial assistance he could.
Eventually two merchants of Irish extraction, Walter Ruttledge of
Dunkirk and Antoine Walsh of Nantes, were engaged to help the Prince.
They had been carrying on with the French government's approval a
profitable *guerre de course* on British merchant ships; they were persuaded to put at the disposal of the Prince two vessels which they had
recently hired from the French government. Besides his services, Walsh
offered the *Du Teillay*[1] an eighteen-gun light frigate named after the
Commissaire de la Marine at Nantes, and Ruttledge provided the sixty-
four gun *Elisabeth* which had been captured from the British. The
change of purpose of the two ships from commerce raiding required the
approval of the Comte de Maurepas, minister for the navy, but Lord
Clare and Antoine Walsh between them achieved this and also persuaded the minister to provide from the French service two captains[2] and
the 'Compagnie Maurepas' which consisted of sixty volunteer officers
and cadets to supplement the crew of the *Elisabeth*.

While preparations for the expedition were in progress Charles
stayed as the guest of the Duc de Bouillon at his Château de Navarre.
From Navarre Charles wrote to King Louis telling him of the coming
attempt, and asking for *'secours médiocre'* to make success certain, which
he felt *'mon oncle ne me refusera pas'*. He also wrote to his father's
secretary saying he had bought arms and ammunition and twenty small
cannon and had obtained two ships and the services of Antoine Walsh of
Nantes. Finally he wrote to his father saying that he hoped, as James
had gone himself in 1715, that he would not disapprove 'a son following

1. *Contracted to* Doutelle *by Johnstone, Chambers and others.*
2. *Captain Durbé and Captain d'Eau.*

the example of his father'; he explained that he had not let his father into the secret before for fear of not being allowed to leave, and he added that although he was writing from Navarre, he would not send off the letter until he was on shipboard, when it would be too late to recall him.

Prince Charles took only a few people into his confidence and selected even fewer to accompany him. In the interests of secrecy he ordered his companions to go to Nantes individually and take up residence in different parts of the town; and he told them that if they met in the streets they must pretend not to recognize one another. On 20 June, 1745, when all was ready, he left Navarre for Nantes, proceeded to its outpost Saint-Nazaire, and on 21 June went on board the *Du Teillay*. The members[1] of his suite who joined him were the Marquis of Tullibardine, Sir Thomas Sheridan, George Kelly, Colonel Strickland, Aeneas Macdonald, and from the French service Sir John Macdonald and Colonel O'Sullivan. There were also Mr. Buchanan, Aeneas Macdonald's steward, and, in a humbler position, Duncan Cameron, sometime servant to old Lochiel. Duncan was a native of Barra, and had been specially engaged for the purpose of securing someone to pilot them among the dangerous rocks and shoals of the islands of the Outer Hebrides where the first landing in Scotland was planned to take place.

From Saint-Nazaire the two ships moved westwards and anchored near Belle Isle off the mouth of the Loire; then on 5 July they sailed with a fair wind. The voyage was without incident until 120 miles west of the Brittany coast, when following a day of dead calm, a sail was seen to windward which proved to be the *Lion*, a British man-o'-war of sixty guns commanded by Captain Brett. Prince Charles was just preparing to transfer from the *Du Teillay* to the *Elisabeth*, where accommodation was better, when the sight of the British ship made him change his mind. Instead, Captain d'Eau of *Elisabeth* came aboard *Du Teillay* to confer with Antoine Walsh and Captain Durbé as to what was best to be done. It was decided that the *Elisabeth* should approach the enemy and, having received the first broadside, deliver her own and proceed to board. Captain d'Eau suggested that the *Du Teillay* should support her; but Antoine Walsh, who had assumed command over everyone, including the Prince, refused because it was too risky with such an important passenger aboard. Meanwhile the *Lion* had drawn closer to the *Elisabeth*, and before Captain d'Eau, his sword drawn ready to lead the boarding party, had climbed aboard, his Lieutenant, oblivious of what had just been planned, lowered the long-boat, hauled up the courses, hoisted the French flag and delivered the first broadside.

The French fire was instantly returned by the *Lion*, on which the *Elisabeth* lowered her courses again and made sail to swing round and

1. *Later known as the Men of Moidart, where they landed.*

I. GEORGE II AT DETTINGEN: THE DUKE OF
CUMBERLAND FOUGHT ALONGSIDE HIS FATHER AND
'JUST AS BRAVELY'. HE IS THE LAST MOUNTED FIGURE
ON THE RIGHT.
By John Wootton

2. KING LOUIS, THE DAUPHIN AND OLD MARSHAL DE
SAXE AT FONTENOY.
By Lenfant

Tullibardine as a young man. He crossed from France with Charles in Du Teillay

15

The battle between the Lion *and the* Elisabeth *off Brest while* Du Teillay, *with the Prince aboard, was on the way to Scotland. By Samuel Scott*

give the *Lion* her other side; but before she could do so, the *Lion* tacked about and poured in another broadside more deadly than the first which raked the *Elisabeth* fore and aft and killed a number of men including Captain d'Eau. The French ship, however, succeeded for her part in disabling the *Lion*. She shot clear away her mizzen, and brought down most of her sails and rigging, and in a subsequent report to the Admiralty Captain Brett said, 'We received a great many shots in our hull which killed 45 men and disabled 107 more with wounds.' However, in spite of this destructive start the two ships continued battering each other for several hours until nightfall when as if by mutual consent they drew away. Prince Charles had been greatly concerned that his vessel had contributed nothing during the fight and had implored Antoine Walsh to let the *Du Teillay* join in. This Walsh positively refused to do. He even threatened to order the Prince to his cabin unless he stopped badgering him.

When the action had petered out the Prince's party went over to see the damage and receive from the Lieutenant a report of the *Elisabeth*'s losses. Fifty-seven had been killed, they learnt, and a hundred and seventy-six were wounded; moreover the damage to the hull was so serious that the vessel could clearly not continue the voyage: it was even doubtful if she would make Brest in safety. Obviously the arms she carried and the 'Compagnie Maurepas', seven of whom had been killed, were lost to the expedition. The Lieutenant did offer to continue if

16

supplied with a main-mast and some rigging, but Antoine Walsh would not spare anything. He ordered the *Elisabeth*, whatever the danger of sinking, to return to Brest, and decided courageously to sail his own little frigate on to Scotland. The two Macdonalds and Colonel Strickland had advised the Prince to make for Nantes and await the refitting of the *Elisabeth*, or arrange for another ship to take her place; but Charles gratefully accepted Antoine Walsh's offer to continue, for he believed that success was still possible even without the *Elisabeth* and her precious cargo. To all objections raised he merely replied, 'You'll see. It will be all right.'

The *Du Teillay* thus proceeded on her course alone, but every precaution was taken by her navigator Captain Durbé to avoid the attentions of other British ships on patrol. A sharp look-out was kept at all times, and at night no lights were allowed except for the compass. On 11 July a vessel did give chase for some time, but being less speedy than the *Du Teillay* was soon left behind. The *Du Teillay* encountered rough seas and gale-force winds on the 15th and 16th, after which the weather was fine until the 20th when they had to ride out another gale. On the 22nd, in better weather again, they came at last within sight of land. The long dark shape on the horizon was what the locals call Long Island because it seems on approaching to be one island whereas in reality it is the necklace of islands forming the Outer Hebrides: Lewis, the Uists, Barra and the rest. According to Captain Durbé's log they made for the east of Long Island and anchored off the coast of Barra, the territory of the McNeils, one of whose chiefs, Roderick McNeil, was the brother-in-law of Aeneas Macdonald. When the long-boat had been lowered, Aeneas Macdonald along with Duncan Cameron was rowed across the bay to the castle of Kisimal on its rocky islet. Neither had much success, as Aeneas found that his brother-in-law was away from home, and Duncan Cameron only managed to bring back Barra's piper who was an old acquaintance, useful to provide the martial strains of the pibroch, but of little value as a pilot. The news that they heard on Barra was hardly encouraging: the Government had arrested the chief of the Macleans of Mull, a prominent Jacobite plotter, which suggested that the Prince's design had been discovered.

According to Durbé's journal, at this stage there was a general feeling that it was not worth going on, though neither the Prince nor Antoine Walsh shared that view. Then they spied a big ship tacking off shore, her topsail close-reefed. Taking her to be an enemy man-of-war, they quickly decided to sail away and seek a safer anchorage among the islands between Barra and South Uist. They found a suitable reach, but almost immediately the sinister vessel loomed up again, so they up-anchored once more and sailed right round to the west coast of Eriskay. Consisting of a few square miles of rocky hill rising out of the sea the island had few inhabitants, and was owned by Alexander of Boisdale, another member of the Macdonald clan. Colonel O'Sullivan records that 'it was blowing hard and there was a cruel rain', but before landing they saw something they interpreted as a favourable omen. An eagle[1] was circling the sky above their heads, and Tullibardine pointed it out to the Prince saying that it was a good sign that the king of birds had come to welcome him.

They landed in a beautiful sandy bay, later named appropriately 'Prince's Strand', and believed they had found a remote enough spot until they saw two other ships passing at no great distance; then they promptly decided to make their stay on Eriskay a short one. All the principals except Tullibardine who was suffering from gout had gone ashore despite the weather. They took shelter first in a bothy. Here Duncan, having failed to find a pilot[2], and not having contributed much so far, showed his worth by cooking over a peat fire some flounders for them to eat. This put the Prince in very good spirits, and he sat himself down on a heap of peat near the door, and laughed and chatted, and teased Duncan Cameron about his cooking. Soon, however, they moved inland to seek better quarters for the night, and were finally accommodated in the home of a Macdonald tenant who was the proud possessor of a few good beds. There were not enough for them all, and the Prince surrendered his to Sir Thomas Sheridan. He seems to have been particularly mindful of the comfort of his beloved old tutor on this occasion, as he apparently inspected the sheets for vermin before handing the bed over, much to the annoyance of his host who called out that he need not trouble as it was a good one and fit for a prince (the Prince was *incognito*, in the garb of an Irish priest, and the man's comment suggests he may have recognized him).

The island of Eriskay lay next to the territory of the fifteenth Macdonald chief of Clanranald; but although only fifty-three years old, he was infirm. His son Clanranald the younger who lived on the mainland was the most likely person to win over the Macdonalds to Prince Charles; but both the old chief and Sir Alexander Macdonald of Boisdale, his brother, were on South Uist nearby, so a message was immediately sent to Sir Alexander asking him to come over to Eriskay to confer. He was not slow to obey this summons, and next morning, when they had returned to the *Du Teillay*, he was rowed over from the island and came aboard. It soon became clear that he was not going to be helpful, for he spoke 'in a very discouraging manner to the Prince and advised him to go home'. To which the Prince replied, 'I am come home, sir, and I will entertain no notion at all of returning from where I came, for

1. *Some authorities give this incident before the landing on the mainland.*
2. *But Forbes writes, 'The piper piloted them safely to Eriskay;' so he may have been useful.*

I am persuaded my faithful Highlanders will stand by me.' Charles then asked him to approach the Skye chiefs, but Sir Alexander firmly refused to do so, saying that Macdonald of Sleat and the chief of the Macleods had told him that they would not leave Skye to take part in any uprising which lacked French support, and that if the Prince arrived without French troops they would advise him to return. While this discussion was in progress, two ships appeared over the horizon, a big man-of-war, similar to the one that had previously alarmed them, and a frigate. Although well out to sea, it was feared they were coming in to attack, so Sir Alexander Macdonald, still adamant in his opposition, was put ashore, and Captain Durbé took his ship quietly out of the anchorage under a sprit-sail until he reached the Minch. Then he crowded on sail and made for the mainland. Next morning they sailed into Loch-nan-Uamh which was to become an important anchorage during the '45 uprising. Lying between the Inverness-shire districts of Arisaig and Moidart, both Macdonald territories, Loch-nan-Uamh was a suitable area from which to approach young Clanranald, nephew of the unhelpful Sir Alexander, and Macdonald of Kinlochmoidart, brother of Aeneas Macdonald; as well as being close to the territories of Clan Cameron, and the Macdonells of Glengarry and of Keppoch who are included like the Clanranalds in the Clan Donald.

Prince Charles remained on board the *Du Teillay* until 25 July, spending his last days despatching messages to chiefs of clans he thought would support him, including Donald Cameron, leader of the mighty Camerons. Then he landed on the north shore of Loch-nan-Uamh and took up his abode at Borrodale. At this juncture the arms, ammunition and stores from the holds of the *Du Teillay* were landed, and Antoine Walsh took his leave. Captain Durbé in his journal writes that several gentlemen of the country came aboard, and he asked them where the best place was to unload the arms. He was told on the shore of Loch Ailort by the lower slopes of Mount Fros-Sheinn in Moidart, so Durbé took his ship there and 'from then until three the following morning the arms were landed'. *Du Teillay* remained in Loch Ailort for eight days, then on 6 August sailed back to Loch-nan-Uamh and took on cattle and sheep for the voyage back to France, while Walsh and Durbé went over to Borrodale to wait on the Prince and wish him good-bye and good luck. The entry in the log of the *Du Teillay* continues with scarcely concealed astonishment: 'We left him with two of the gentlemen, two chiefs of the district, and with no more than a dozen men – these being all his companions.' Antoine Walsh had served the Prince well, and was handsomely rewarded. Charles dubbed him a knight, gave him a gold-hilted sword and a sum of money, and sent a letter to his father suggesting that for his services Walsh should be created 'Comte d'Irlande', adding, *'C'est la première grâce que je vous demande depuis mon arrivée dans ce pays.'*

Charles with Antoine Walsh, who brought him to Scotland

20

Chapter III

GLENFINNAN

'I'll share the fate of my Prince,' exclaimed Lochiel, 'and so shall every man over whom nature or fortune has given me any power.'

HOME

Prince Charles found it difficult to persuade the Macdonald and Cameron chiefs to support the Stuart cause, as is evidenced by the story of how eventually he won over Young Clanranald and Young Lochiel. Young Clanranald, Kinlochmoidart and his brother arrived together at Loch-nan-Uamh before the departure of the *Du Teillay*. Reaching Forsy, a small village opposite the anchorage, they signalled for a ship's boat and were rowed over. On deck in a tent erected on poles were tables stacked with flagons of wine, and as they climbed on board, Tullibardine, sparing his gouty foot, hobbled forward cheerfully to greet them. Kinlochmoidart had already expressed his willingness to join the cause, so only Clanranald was asked to descend the companion-way for an audience of the Prince in his cabin, and the others joined the gathering in the booth. Clanranald was with the Prince for over two hours, but does not seem to have been persuaded. On their reappearance they were joined by Kinlochmoidart, and all three paced the deck, the Prince still arguing and cajoling. Kinlochmoidart's brother, armed and in Highland dress, was standing like a sentinel at the top of the companion-way waiting for them, and could not help hearing the gist of their argument as they passed to and fro. For a time he made no move, but at last, unable to hold himself back any longer, he moved forward a pace or two towards them, his eyes sparkling with indignation suggesting that, even if Clanranald would not follow the Prince, he would do so willingly. Charles noticing this, turned hopefully towards the young man. 'Will you assist me then?' he asked. 'I will, I will,' exclaimed the Highlander excitedly. 'Though no other man should draw a sword, I am ready to die for you!' Charles, delighted at receiving this unexpected support, was profuse in his thanks, and said he only wished all the Highlanders were like him. On this Clanranald stirred by what seemed a rebuke, and extremely moved by the young Highlander's example, declared that he too would support the Prince.

After the *Du Teillay* had left, and while the Prince was staying in

Clanranald territory at Borrodale in Arisaig, he was visited by Donald Cameron of Lochiel. Donald Cameron was known as Young Lochiel, because, when his father had been attainted for his part in the 1715 Rebellion, Donald had assumed the leadership of the Camerons. The Prince told him that although he had brought few supplies he had written to the French King asking for '*secours médiocre*'[1] which he fully expected to receive, and he had asked Marischal his agent in France to organise its despatch. It should arrive very soon, he said. But this did not satisfy Lochiel who pointed out that the members of the 1740 Edinburgh association, of which he was one, had agreed to rise and support the Prince only if he brought a French force with him. He thought the Prince should return to France and wait for the French help to materialize before attempting to initiate an uprising. As for himself, he was not prepared to join the present hopeless attempt.

Charles continued to press him to join, emphasizing, with some truth, that the few British troops available to resist him would not be able to withstand the body of Highlanders his friends could bring into the field, and that if he were to win a few early victories, not only would the whole country declare in his favour, but his foreign friends would undoubtedly come and join him. These arguments still had no influence on Lochiel who finding the Prince utterly averse to returning suggested he might send his companions back, remain himself in hiding, and wait while his friends in the Highlands had time to confer and decide what best to do. This Charles refused indignantly to consider. He said he proposed to take the field however small his support might be. 'Soon,' he announced, 'with the few friends that I have, I will raise the royal standard and proclaim to the people that Charles Stuart is come over to claim the crown of his ancestors – to win it, or die in the attempt. Lochiel, whom my father has often told me was our firmest friend, may stay at home, and from the newspapers learn the fate of his prince.' This appeal proved irresistible. 'No!' exclaimed Lochiel. 'I'll share the fate of my prince; and so shall every man over whom nature or fortune has given me any power.'

With some of the Macdonalds, and now the Camerons, pledged to his support Prince Charles's prospects had become much brighter. He decided to raise his standard, and with this in view, sent messages to favourably disposed chiefs to assemble on 19 August at Glenfinnan. Immediately afterwards he left Borrodale and Clanranald's territory, crossed over Loch-nan-Uamh, and went to stay in Moidart with Macdonald of Kinlochmoidart whom he at once offered a colonel's commission and promised a peerage.

1. *French assistance in men and material did eventually arrive in Scotland while the Prince was invading England. One of the reasons why his army turned back at Derby was to join up with these French reinforcements.*

Cameron of Lochiel, 'Young Lochiel', by George Chalmers

During Prince Charles's stay at Kinlochmoidart the clans began to raise their fighting men, and small parties of armed Highlanders started to move about the countryside to their assembly points. This did not escape the notice of the authorities who soon became convinced that an armed uprising was about to take place. Alarmed at reports of Highlanders on the move in the neighbourhood of Fort William, the governor of Fort Augustus sent, on 16 August, two companies of the Royal Scots under Captain Scott to reinforce the garrison. They followed General Wade's military road southwards and met with no interference until they reached High Bridge over the Spean, eight miles from Fort William. The narrow bridge, consisting of one arch, seemed a likely place for an ambush so the conscientious Captain Scott sent forward a sergeant and his own soldier servant to investigate. They had hardly left when bagpipe music was heard in the distance, and then well beyond the bridge Highlanders were seen leaping around and extending

23

their plaids as if to demonstrate how formidable they were. Owing to a dip in the ground they were not visible to the pair advancing to reconnoitre, and these, all unsuspecting, were pounced on, seized and made prisoner by Highlanders who had concealed themselves behind the parapet of the bridge. All this had been watched by the soldiers without any immediate reaction but, after a moment, Captain Scott gathered his wits, made a quick appreciation, and decided that, as he did not know the number of his assailants, he had better retrace his steps. Remounting his horse, he ordered his men to face about, and he led them back the way they had come. The Highlanders were Keppochs, only twelve in number, and their antics before the capture of the two soldiers had been designed to make Scott believe they were far more numerous. Their commander Macdonald of Tierndrech was loth to display his weakness, and let the soldiers go without immediately pursuing them. But he sent messages to Macdonell of Keppoch and Young Lochiel asking for reinforcements.

After a trouble-free march, carried out from time to time at the double-quick, the soldiers came to another dangerous defile, where the road ran along a narrow ledge between Loch Lochy and steep mountains to the east. By this time the Highlanders had caught the soldiers up. Racing round to the east, they climbed the mountains and, from the shelter of the rocks and trees, fired down on the soldiers as they passed below. By pressing his men forward, Captain Scott escaped this trap; only to be confronted by another party of Highlanders perched on a hill commanding the road ahead towards Loch Oich. Blocked in front and behind, Scott now turned westwards across the isthmus between Loch Lochy and Loch Oich with the intention of seeking refuge for his men in Invergarry Castle, the seat of Macdonell of Glengarry. It was a vain move, for the Macdonells were now supporters of the Prince, indeed a party of Macdonells was soon seen marching aggressively towards them. Hemmed in now on three sides Captain Scott rejoined the military road leading north and formed his men into a hollow square to fight it out. It proved a hopeless proposition, for there were now many armed Highlanders all round: two parties of Macdonells of Glengarry ahead and Tierndrech's men reinforced by more Macdonells of Keppoch behind. By this time Scott had been wounded, and had had two men killed, so when Macdonell of Keppoch approached him and offered generous terms he agreed to surrender. At that moment Lochiel arrived with a party of his Camerons, and he was given the task of taking the prisoners back to his home at Achnacarry which was not far away. Meanwhile, Captain Scott was released on parole and his horse taken by Tierndrech to present to the Prince.

The news of the clansmen's success was received with delight by Prince Charles and his companions, who hailed it as a harbinger of certain success for their venture. Nor was it the only one, as soon afterwards Captain Sweetenham of Guise's Regiment[1] was brought to him as a prisoner; he had been taken at an inn by some of Keppoch's men as he was on his way to visit Fort William. Prince Charles now left Kinlochmoidart for Glenaladale, the seat of Alexander Macdonald, on the western shore of Loch Shiel five miles south of Glenfinnan, the place chosen for the raising of the standard. The following day he took a boat up Loch Shiel and landed at the head of the loch, where he was met by 150 Macdonalds. He had expected to find many more Highlanders who had answered his call, but the only others at the landing place were the inhabitants of bothies scattered about the glen. In despair he chose a handy hut and went there with his retinue to await, not very hopefully, the arrival of further clansmen. The Prince and his staff were sitting gloomily in the darkness of the windowless building when they heard in the distance the intermittent sound of bagpipes. They listened carefully, and as time passed, the sounds became clearer. Running outside, they now saw a dark mass coming over the hills into the glen. It was the Clan Cameron, between 700 and 800 of them, with Young Lochiel at their head; and, as their columns came nearer, the soldiers taken in the recent scuffle could be seen marching as captives within their ranks.

Elated by this happy sight, Prince Charles declared that he would raise his standard and declare open war on George II and his supporters without waiting for the other clans he had been expecting to join him. He therefore called on Tullibardine to proceed with the ceremony. The Marquis with two supporters took the white, blue and red silk flag up on to the top of a small knoll, and, having raised it on high, proceeded to read, first a proclamation from James appointing his son as his regent, and then a manifesto declaring their intentions. Having sympathized with the miseries they had suffered under Hanoverian rule, during which their country had been garrisoned by troops as if it were hostile, the manifesto outlined the benefits the Stuarts would bring: pardon for those who had in the past supported the Hanoverian regime; promises of a free parliament, and the enjoyment by all, including Protestants, of liberty and freedom. Finally sheriffs and magistrates were required to proclaim the manifesto at the market crosses of their respective county towns and boroughs.

After reading the manifesto, Tullibardine returned to the hut with the standard escorted by fifty Camerons, and soon afterwards all the Prince's gloomy forebodings were dispelled. First, Macdonell of Keppoch appeared with 300 clansmen; these were followed by a party of Macleods from Skye whose leaders said they disagreed with the policy of their uncooperative chief and were willing to return to Skye and raise

---

1. *The 6th of Foot (later the Royal Warwicks).*

more men; and finally, Tierndrech arrived bringing Captain Scott's captured charger which he presented to the Prince. Now clansmen filled the glen, bagpipe music sounded all around, and Prince Charles found himself, within a few hours, at the head of 1,200 men warmly attached to him and his cause.

Chapter IV

RUTHVEN

Cope in forwarding a copy of Sergeant Molloy's report to the Horse Guards called him 'a very good sergeant' and recommended him for a commission.

STATE PAPERS

By a coincidence General Sir John Cope assembled his troops at Stirling to deal with the Highland uprising on 19 August, 1745, the same day that Prince Charles had raised the standard at Glenfinnan. George II was in Hanover and the affairs of his kingdom were in the hands of the Lords Justices. These included for Scotland Lord Tweeddale, the Duke of Argyll and Duncan Forbes of Culloden. Early in July Duncan Forbes, who although Lord President and a Government supporter had many friends among the Highland chiefs, showed Cope a letter which he had received mentioning a proposed uprising. Cope passed on the information to Tweeddale from whom it went to the Duke of Newcastle in London; as a result it was ruled that Wade's forts should be strengthened and the loyal clans armed. Guise's Regiment was sent to reinforce the forts, but the loyal clans were only employed to a limited degree, for some held the view that it was unwise to arm loyal Highlanders. Lord Chesterfield, the Lord-Lieutenant of Ireland, when asked to supply oatmeal for them, flatly refused, and said in a letter to the Duke of New-castle: 'I am very sorry to hear that loyal Highlanders are to be armed at all. The proverb indeed says, "Set a thief to catch a thief," but I beg leave to except Scotch thieves, for I believe that those to whom money is given to raise loyal Highlanders will put that money in their pockets and not raise a man.' The Duke of Argyll, leader of the largest loyal clan, thought that he should have been given the task of keeping the peace in the Highlands, and had been upset when his rival Lord Tweeddale had been made Secretary of State for Scotland; but both Tweeddale and Duncan Forbes, who had hurried north to Culloden to organise well-affected clans, were of the opinion that arming the Campbells would lead to a civil war between them and traditional enemies, so, to start with, only some additional independent companies of Black Watch were enrolled under Lord John Murray, and a Highland regiment embodied under Lord Loudoun.

There were 3,000 regular troops in Scotland, but for his march north

Duncan Forbes, Lord President, who lived at Culloden House and tried to keep the peace in the Highlands. Attributed to Jeremiah Davison

Cope managed to assemble at Stirling no more than 1,400. He got off to a slow start even when the news of Prince Charles's arrival in Scotland was confirmed. Officers had to be recalled from leave, and as no food was available in the country through which he intended to march, cattle on the hoof had to be collected and bread and biscuit procured. Cope bought up all the biscuit which the bakers of Edinburgh and Leith had and set them and those at Perth and Stirling to work night and day to bake sufficient bread to last his army twenty-one days.[1] Only part of this had come to hand by 19 August, so he set off with the limited amount he had received and gave orders for the remainder to be brought up when he reached Stirling. The route he chose followed Wade's military road by Crieff, Tay Bridge (Aberfeldy), Dalnacardoch and Dalwhinnie to Fort Augustus. It crossed the Monadhliath Range at the Carriearrack Pass where Wade had constructed on the south side a series of wide hairpin bends which quadrupled the travelling distance across.

Cope marched north from Stirling with Lee's[2] and Murray's regiments, two companies of Black Watch, four small field guns, four mortars, and a wagon train 'so large as to impede his movements'.[3] He left his two regiments of dragoons in the Stirling area as he considered they would be no use in a campaign among the mountains, but he took 1,000 stand of spare arms with the intention of arming well-disposed Highlanders. Cope halted on 21 August at Crieff where Lascelles's Regiment[4] joined bringing the additional supplies of bread. Duncan Forbes on his way north to pacify the clans had appointed Lord George Murray deputy-sheriff of Perthshire with instructions to provide Cope with 'everything required that the county can provide', and Lord George was at Crieff to greet the general. Among other chiefs there were Murray's brother Duke James of Atholl, and John Macdonell of Invergarry. Cope said that if they raised their men they could have some of the additional arms he was carrying. They all demurred for one reason or another, except Atholl who provided a very small force most of whom later deserted. There now seemed no further use for the large quantity of spare arms, and Cope sent them back to Stirling. So disgusted was he at the chiefs' poor support that, if he had not received strict orders from the Lords Justices to proceed north without delay, he would have returned to Stirling. His difficulties increased as the march continued. His baggage horses strayed at night and hours were wasted rounding them up; and the men of Lord John Murray's Black Watch companies started to desert. However, at Tay Bridge he was joined by a contingent of Lord Loudoun's Highlanders which was some compensa-

1. *Cope's Trial.*
2. *44th, later Essex.*
3. *Fortescue.*
4. *47th, later N. Lancs.*

Duke James of Atholl by Allan Ramsay

tion. On 22 August he reached Dalnacardoch and was met by Captain Sweetenham who had been released on parole. Sweetenham told the general that there had been 1,400 Highlanders at Glenfinnan, and on his way back he had seen many Highland parties on the move westward; he estimated the present strength of the rebels at 3,000. He said Prince Charles's force was making for the Carriearrack Pass and intended to meet Cope there and give battle.

Prince Charles and his clansmen marched eastwards from Glenfinnan along the north shore of Loch Eil and almost at once ran into trouble, for the track was so bad that the cannon got stuck, and they were forced to bury some pieces in the bog for future use. At Kinlocheil during a halt to reorganize the transport, which eventually took a different route, the Prince heard that the British Government had put a price of £30,000 on his head. He countered this with an offer of £30 for the head of the Elector of Hanover, later raising it to the identical sum of £30,000. On 23 August they reached Fassifern, the house of Lochiel's brother John. By rights John should have become second-in-command of the Cameron

3. PIPER OF THE BLACK WATCH AT THE PERIOD OF THE
UPRISING: SOMETIMES ERRONEOUSLY STYLED 'PRINCE
CHARLES'S PIPER'.

4. LORD GEORGE MURRAY, PRINCE CHARLES'S SENIOR
LIEUTENANT-GENERAL.

Lord Loudoun, a Campbell who raised the 64th (Highland) Regiment of Foot and fought on the Government side. By Allan Ramsay

battalion, but he had decided not to support the Prince and was away from home. Charles's stop at Fassifern was not entirely pointless, for in the garden white roses[1] were blooming and tradition has it that he picked one and took it as his symbol, and it became the basis of the White Cockade emblem of the '45.

After a detour to escape the guns of a British warship lying off Fort William (which the baggage train had to face by the shore route, though without mishap) they came to Loch Lochy, and half-way up the eastern shore received a report saying that Cope was marching through the Perthshire Highlands on his way to Fort Augustus and intended to cross the Monadhliath Range by the Carriearrack Pass. This news caused the march north to be speeded up, and the next stop was at Invergarry Castle on the west shore of Loch Oich, the home of John Macdonell who had attended Cope at Crieff. Macdonell's Glengarry clansmen, however, were not to follow their chief's example, for 450 joined the Prince, and their leaders invited him to spend a night in the

1. Rosa alba semi-plana, *a variety which still grows at Fassifern.*

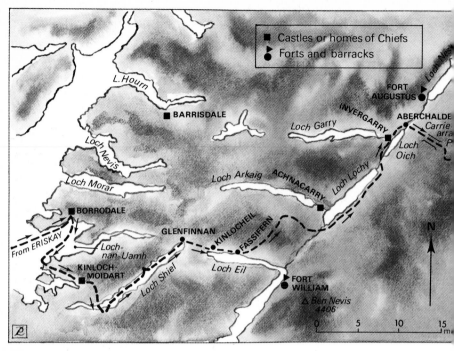

The Raising of the Clans and the March South

castle, from which Glengarry contingents had started to join Bonnie Dundee in 1685 and the Earl of Mar in 1715. About this time 260 Stewarts of Appin also arrived. Spirits were high among the Prince's supporters at Invergarry that night, and, after a banquet in the hall, a conference was held. A message had just been received from Lord Lovat with excuses for not putting the Frasers in readiness, and pleading the close proximity of the garrisons at Inverness and Fort Augustus which made warlike preparations impossible without giving notice to the enemy. He had suggested he would join the Prince if created a duke and appointed a lieutenant-general. Nevertheless, although the appointments had been confirmed he had made no move, and he was clearly waiting to pick the winning side. When they began to discuss plans for the forth-coming campaign, Lord Lovat's messenger said that if they marched northwards, the Frasers would rise to a man, as would the Grants and other clans of the north-east; but Tullibardine did not agree and suggested instead that they should advance only as far as Aberchalder at the north-eastern end of Loch Oich, then turn and cross the Monadh-liath Range and offer battle to Cope in the foothills on the far side where a strong defensive position would be found. Tullibardine added that if

32

Wine glasses engraved with the White Rose which became the Jacobite emblem along with the white cockade or a knotted white ribbon

they stopped on the way south at Blair Castle strong reinforcements could be had from the Murrays, Stewarts and Robertsons of Atholl despite the Whig sympathies of his brother Duke James. If this were followed by the seizure of Edinburgh, the news that the capital was in their hands would bring a flood of supporters to the cause. After some discussion, the bolder plan with its prospect of immediate battle won the support of the majority of the chiefs, and it was decided to march next day to Aberchalder, halt there one day to allow all the stragglers to come up, and then cross the mountains and prepare to meet Cope's army.

An early start was made and Charles 'in top spirits and eager for a fight' delighted his army by appearing in 'Highland Cloaths' for the first time since he had been in Scotland. Nothing could exceed the wildness and grandeur of the scenery by which they were surrounded.

33

In front barring the way stood the mighty hills of Monadhliath, their cloud-wreathed peaks rearing almost 3,000 feet into the sky, and mountain torrents tumbled down over lichen-covered boulders between wide sweeps of their heather-covered slopes. From the summit of the pass they expected to see Cope's redcoats making their way towards them. But no one was in sight. When, however, they had advanced cautiously by Wade's zig-zags half-way down on the other side of the range they noticed a body of armed Highlanders in the distance. As the clansmen approached it appeared by their demeanour that they were not hostile, and when they came up it was found that they were deserters from Cope's army. And they had some surprising news. Apparently, when Cope reached Dalwhinnie two days before he had called a council of war at which it was decided not to proceed over the Carriearrack Pass to Fort Augustus, but instead to turn north-eastwards up the valley of the Spey towards Ruthven and Inverness. Some of the chiefs wanted to go after Cope, but when it was discovered that he had already passed Ruthven and that it would require a march of twenty-four miles to catch him, it was decided not to follow with the whole force but to send instead a detachment of Camerons to capture Ruthven barracks.

The garrison at Ruthven consisted of twelve men from Guise's Regiment under Sergeant Molloy; and they resisted the Highland attack gallantly. According to Molloy's report[1] to General Cope 300 surrounded the barracks and demanded the surrender of the men of the garrison, on which they could move out unharmed with their bag and baggage. When Molloy replied that he was too old a soldier to surrender a strong garrison 'without bloody noses', the Highlanders threatened to hang him and his men, but Molloy said he would take his chance. The report continues: 'This morning they attacked me with about a hundred and fifty men: they attacked the foregate and sally-port and attempted to set the sally-port on fire with some old barrels and other combustibles which took blaze immediately, but the attempter lost his life by it. They drew off and later sent word that two of their chiefs[2] wanted to talk to me. I spoke to them from the parapet; they offered conditions, I refused: they desired liberty to carry off their dead men; I granted. They went off westward about eight o'clock this morning . . . they took all the provisions the poor inhabitants had from them, and Mrs. Mcpherson, the barrack-wife, and a merchant of the town who spoke to me this moment, advised me to write to your honour. Both told me there were above 3,000 men all lodged in the cornfields west of the town last night, and their grand camp is at Dalwhinnie. They have taken Cluny Mcpherson prisoner with them as I have it by the same information. I lost

1. State papers, Scotland, Series II, 25.
2. Possibly Dr. Cameron and Colonel O'Sullivan.

Drum of the 6th Regiment of Foot (Guise's) to which both the gallant Sergeant Molloy of Ruthven and the ruthless Captain Caroline Scott belonged. The drum was captured during the uprising and recovered later

one man shot through the head by foolishly holding it too high over the parapet contrary to orders. I prevented the sally-port taking fire by pouring water over the parapet. I expect another visit this night, but I shall give them the warmest reception my weak party can afford. I shall hold out as long as possible.' Inspired by their staunch leader the little garrison did hold out; and eventually the Camerons went off back to rejoin the main body at Dalwhinnie, taking Cluny with them as prisoner.

Blair Castle, home of the Dukes of Atholl

This brought the Highlanders their only gain from the abortive attack, for after a long interview with the Prince, Cluny was released on promising to raise his clan.

On the following day they marched to Castle Blair of which, as it had been abandoned by Duke James, his attainted brother Tullibardine took possession so as to entertain the Prince. At Blair they were joined by Lord Nairne, but most of the local gentry had fled on the approach of the Highland army. They next proceeded slowly towards Perth, stopping at several places on the way. The entry into Perth was made into something of a ceremony by the Prince who dressed himself in a suit of tartan trimmed with gold lace and rode in at the head of his men on the horse taken by Tierndrech from Captain Scott. Charles is said to have set up his headquarters in the inn which is now the Salutation Hotel, and as his privy purse contained a solitary guinea one of the first things he did was to set about improving his finances by demanding a contribution of £500 from the provost and bailies of Perth. This they generously agreed to make on condition that the citizens and their goods were not interfered with. From Perth some clansmen marched to Dundee to proclaim King James VIII and obtain additional support; and they managed to seize in the harbour a ship containing a valuable supply of gunpowder which they put under sail to Perth.

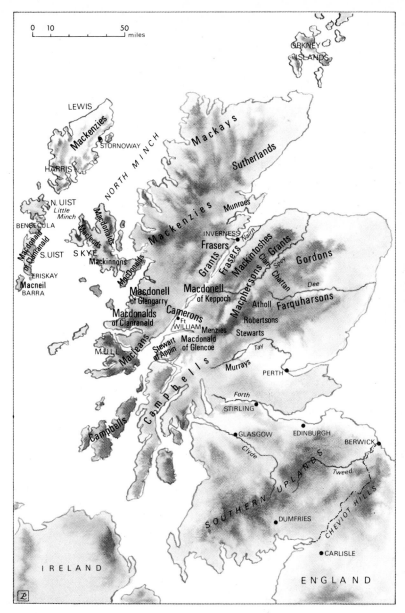

The Clans

At Perth, a number of chiefs joined, some of whom received important appointments in the Highland army along with members of the Prince's personal staff. The Duke of Perth, who was not a claniate chief but leader of the Drummonds, Macgregors and others, was appointed a

37

lieutenant-general; Chevalier Johnstone was made an ADC – and was to write an account of the campaign; Lord Strathallan, a Drummond like the Duke of Perth, was given command of the cavalry; Colonel O'Sullivan was made quartermaster-general, and Sir John Macdonald appointed inspector of cavalry; finally Lord George Murray, who had at last opted for the Stuart cause, was made the other lieutenant-general. Lord George was to play a prominent part in the 1745 adventure. A Jacobite officer described him as 'tall and robust and brave in the highest degree; and always the first to rush sword in hand into the midst of a charge. He slept little, was continually occupied with all manner of details, and was altogether most indefatigable, combining and directing alone all our operations: in a word, he was the only person capable of conducting our army'. However, from the first he was treated with suspicion by the Prince's secretary, Murray of Broughton, and also by O'Sullivan, with whom he quarrelled constantly. They knew that he had gone to greet Cope at Crieff, and had accepted the office of deputy-sheriff from the Lord President. He had been 'out' with his brother Tullibardine in 1719, it is true, but he had since been pardoned and was reckoned a Government supporter. His new comrades, in fact, found it difficult to trust him.

The Duke of Perth managed to enroll 150 Drummonds and Mac-gregors, and Tullibardine brought in some Murrays, Stewarts and Robertsons. The Robertsons or Clan Donnachaidh were not 'out' as a whole in the '45 as they had been in 1715, but by the orders of their veteran chief Struan 140 were mustered, and served throughout the campaign under Donald Robertson of Woodsheal. On meeting Prince Charles at Perth, Struan[1] exclaimed: 'Sir, I devoted my youth to the service of your father and now I devote my old age to your Royal Highness' – on which the sensitive Prince with tears in his eyes embraced the aged chief of the Robertsons.

Charles's departure from Perth was hastened by the receipt of news that General Cope was marching from Inverness to Aberdeen with the intention of embarking his men and sailing to the Firth of Forth to protect Edinburgh. At a council of war two alternative plans were discussed. The first was to proceed northwards by forced marches to try to intercept Cope; the second envisaged an immediate march south on the capital in order to arrive before Cope could reinforce its slender garrison. It did not take long to decide on the latter plan, and the advance was set in stage immediately – though it was not so hurried that Prince Charles was unable to find time to visit en route both Scone Palace, the home of the early Scottish kings, and Doune Castle, which was destined to become a prison for Government soldiers captured by the Jacobites.

1. *Struan brought with him the clan charm – see Appendix B.*

Struan Robertson, the old chief who always took his clan charm stone to the wars. He was present at Prestonpans where some of his clan fought for the Prince

The route south passed through Gask and Lord George Murray's lands at Tullibardine. At Gask the 'auld laird' greeted them warmly, but announced with disappointment that, in spite of strenuous efforts, he had been powerless to raise his clan. At Tullibardine they were entertained lavishly; Sir John Macdonald too lavishly, for, seemingly slightly drunk, he abused Lord George for not providing him with a better mount. Colonel O'Sullivan also had one of his many disputes with Lord George at Tullibardine. As quartermaster-general he had been left behind at Perth to clear up matters after the army had marched, and, finding that the postmaster's wife had not paid twenty pounds due, took prisoner the provost and a bailie and brought them as hostages to Tullibardine House. Lord George was inclined to let the matter drop as most of the £500 asked for had been paid; but Sir Thomas Sheridan supported O'Sullivan in insisting that the officials would be held until the £20 were disgorged. Finally, the matter was brought to the Prince, who on this occasion supported Lord George and allowed the provost and bailie to return.

39

From Tullibardine House they proceeded to Dunblane, and then to Auchterarder where a review was held, described in a paper dated 13 September, 1745, endorsed Intelligence from Scotland.[1]

The army, according to the paper, consisted of 4,000 men, though it is known at this stage to have been only 2,000-strong which casts doubt on the accuracy of the whole report. But in fact what follows may very well be correct. The middle rank, it says, carried only broadswords; those in the other ranks who had guns had no swords, and there were some with only Lochaber axes or scythes. The boys and old men accompanying the baggage train were unarmed. As it is known that during their stay at Perth every effort was made to get targes manufactured and swords provided, this seems a disappointing result.

Jacobite sword

At Doune a pleasant incident occurred which shows how attractive the Prince was to the fair sex. A party of ladies lined the garden wall of Newton House to watch the Highlanders pass. When Charles rode up, they offered refreshment, and although he declined to enter the house he drank a glass of wine brought by 'a daughter of the owner'. After he had finished the girl begged leave to kiss his hand, a favour readily granted. A cousin now appeared, and, being bolder, begged permission 'to pree the Prince's mou'. This expression was unknown to him; but when it was explained, he picked her off the ground and gave her not one but a dozen kisses on the lips.

The Highland army crossed the River Forth by the fords of Frew near Kippen and then skirted Stirling to keep out of range of the Castle's guns. One of the dragoon regiments left by Cope was still in the neighbourhood, but before the Highlanders' advance it fell back towards the other regiment drawn up at Coltbridge near Edinburgh. The Highlanders assembled on the historic field of Bannockburn where a halt was made for them to refresh themselves with bread and cheese and beer sent out from Stirling. Finding the dragoons had halted just beyond the

1. Record Office.

River Avon, a dozen miles or so to the east on the way to Linlithgow and Edinburgh, a body of men, to be led by the Prince himself, was selected to move forward under cover of darkness to catch them by surprise. Although well conceived, this operation came to nothing, for on arrival at the bridge over the Avon it was discovered that the dragoons had decamped. Alarmed at the rapid advance of the Highlanders, they had ridden back to join their fellows at Coltbridge.

On 15 September both regiments were drawn up under Colonel Gardiner for an inspection by a senior officer from Edinburgh. 'Horses soft from having recently been out at grass; many animals' backs too sore to receive riders; officers and men equally unsoldierlike,' were some of his comments. On receiving the adverse report, General Guest, in command at the Castle, sent instructions for the dragoons to join General Cope's army which had just landed at Dunbar twenty miles east of Edinburgh. The dragoons, however, did not receive this order until the Highlanders were upon them.

Meanwhile the main body of the Highland army having passed through Falkirk was approaching Linlithgow. Here the Provost, to avoid compromising himself in the eyes of the Government, retired; but his wife and daughter remained to welcome the Prince. Clad in tartan dresses and wearing the white cockade of the Stuarts in their hats, the ladies received Charles at the Cross, and amid cheers accompanied him to the palace, where a meal had been prepared by Mrs. Glen Gordon, a staunch old Jacobite gentlewoman to whom the care of the building was entrusted.

The following morning the advance began early, with the cavalry ahead, and 'the men drawn up with closed files six in front ready to withstand an attack at a moment's notice'. As the van approached within gun-shot of Edinburgh Castle the officers riding ahead came up with the dragoons at Coltbridge, and drawing their pistols, opened fire on them. According to a tradition not entirely confirmed this was sufficient to cause such panic among the troopers that they turned as one man, and putting spurs to their horses, first galloped straight down the line of present-day George Street, and then on and on towards the welcoming arms of 'Hey Johnny Cope', in what has come to be called 'The Coltbridge Canter'. Edinburgh was thus left unprotected by the regular troops and could be assaulted by the Highlanders at their leisure.

Chapter V

EDINBURGH

A gentleman taking his usual walk on the ramparts noticed with surprise a plaided Highlander sitting astride one of the newly-placed guns. 'Surely you are not one of the same troops who mounted guard here yesterday,' he exclaimed. 'Och no!' replied the Gael. 'They've been relieved.'

NORRIE

There was consternation in Edinburgh when news was received of the Highlanders' advance, for the defences of the city were so flimsy and the men available to man them so inexperienced that, to many of its citizens, any attempts at resistance seemed hopeless. The Castle with its guns and garrison of two companies of Lascelles's Regiment was almost impregnable; but the city itself was very poorly protected. The only defence on the long north side was North Loch, the sheet of water since drained to form the sunken gardens south of Princes Street. Along the southern flank the far-from-solid walls had houses built in them through which entry could be made. As for manpower, other than the regulars in the Castle and the dragoons at Coltbridge there were only the old trained-bands, or such volunteers as could be hastily raised to meet the emergency.

The town council met at once and ordered the gates to be manned and the keys handed to the captain of the guard. Orders also went out for the walls to be repaired, ditches dug, and cannon placed in position. As a number of citizens had offered their services for the defence of their city after authority had been received from London volunteers were enrolled in what came to be called the Edinburgh Regiment. Subscriptions were also accepted to maintain the force, and the response for both men and money was encouraging although, as might be expected considering his name, Lord Provost Stewart appeared rather lukewarm in making the preparations, and less active than ex-Provost Drummond. Drummond busied himself raising volunteers and these he led forth to reinforce for short periods the dragoons outside the town. But even Drummond had his critics, for it was said that with elections approaching he was only out for votes.

All, however, was going quite well until the 'Coltbridge Canter' des-

Plan of Edinburgh

troyed the citizens' confidence. The change it brought about inside Edinburgh is well described in the *History of the Transactions in Scotland* which records: 'A great many of the trained-bands were of the opinion that the city was not tenable; that the sudden flight of the dragoons made it evident that they were of the same opinion; and that if standing out for an hour or two, which was all that could be done, would bring the lives and properties of the inhabitants into certain hazard without doing real service to the cause intended to be served it was certainly more desirable to capitulate on the best terms that could be got.'

At a meeting held in New Church aisle to determine what should be done, and at which the Lord Provost, the ex-Lord Provost, the magistrates and a great number of other people were present, the question was put to the assembled gathering whether they should attempt to defend themselves or not. Meanwhile the volunteers, hearing that the Prince had threatened reprisals against those in Edinburgh found under arms, had on their own initiative begun to deliver their weapons into safe-keeping at the Castle, thus ceasing to be a military force. Noisy from the first, the meeting degenerated into scenes of disorder. The magistrates and other responsible citizens could not get a hearing; shouts of assent and dissent to every proposal rent the air, and everyone appeared to be trying to speak at the same time. At the height of the uproar a man forced his way through the mob to deliver a letter to the Lord Provost. Stewart, finding it was signed, 'Charles P.R.', decided not to open it in the Church, and, having with difficulty closed the meeting, went with the members of the town council to the Goldsmiths' Hall where they could study it in private. In the letter the Prince called upon the council to receive him peacefully into the capital of his father's kingdom of Scotland, and not allow any royal troops to enter, or permit arms and

43

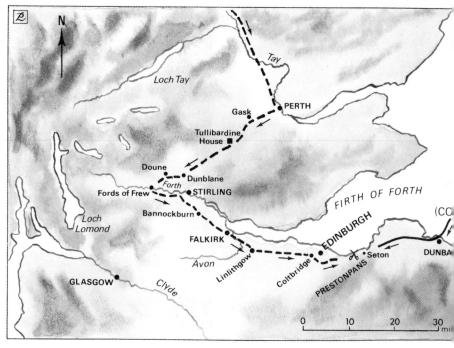

Perth to Prestonpans

ammunition to be removed. He announced that any found under arms would be treated as prisoners of war, but promised that if the citizens co-operated with him he would preserve their liberties and protect their property. This letter, which had been skilfully drawn up by Murray of Broughton, produced the desired effect, for with scarcely a dissentient voice the meeting in Goldsmiths' Hall resolved that as any opposition to the Prince's demands would probably mean the destruction of the town they would offer none. On the other hand, it was decided to send four of the city bailies to beg Prince Charles not to commence hostilities until they had had more time to discuss his demands.

The deputies left the city by West Port about eight o'clock that evening and went on foot to the Highlanders' camp at Slateford a mile or so south-west of the city. On their return they brought a reply from the Prince which reiterated his previous demands and gave them until two o'clock next morning to decide. If they did not agree by then to capitulate he would take the necessary steps to make them conform to his wishes. The deputies also reported that they had been closely questioned as to the whereabouts of the arms served out to the volunteers, and the Prince had not been pleased when they told him they had been taken to the Castle. Although by this time the news of the arrival of Sir John

44

Edinburgh Castle

Cope's army had been received, and confidence somewhat restored, the meeting was still decided on ultimate surrender. There was a flood of talk, though, which continued until the sound of two o'clock clanging from the steeples of the city churches unpleasantly reminded them that their time limit had expired. Hastily they decided to send further envoys to ask for an extension. The five new deputies left for Slateford camp in a coach; but on their arrival were summarily dismissed, and they returned more quickly than they had set out. They noticed at the Highlanders' camp that preparations were being made for a move, and deduced that the threatened assault on the city was about to begin.

The detachment chosen to attack Edinburgh consisted of a thousand men led by Lochiel drawn from Camerons, Glengarries, and Macdonalds. They were promised two shillings each if successful, but were enjoined to treat the citizens with civility and not to get drunk. They marched out soon after the deputies had departed in their coach and, passing, through the southern suburbs, proceeded cautiously along the Pleasance and St. Mary's Wynd to the west end of Canongate near the Netherbow Port where they hid in gardens in the shadow of some tall houses and waited for an opportunity to enter the gate the moment it was opened. They had not met a soul on the way and, although they had distinctly heard the sentries on the castle walls calling the rounds, there were no signs that their approach had been discovered by the garrison. But the gate still remained closed, and daylight was rapidly approaching. Lochiel began to grow impatient, and disguising one of his men in a greatcoat with a hunting cape, and ordering him to demand entrance, he held the rest of his men in readiness to force a passage as soon as the gate was opened. The ruse proved unsuccessful, however, as all admission was being refused by the sentry on duty.

After a further wait it was decided to try to find a better place to gain entry, and a move was just being made when an unlooked-for incident gave them the opportunity they had been seeking. The driver of the coach which had brought back the deputies, having set down his fares at Mrs. Clark's Tavern where the Lord Provost and members of the town council had repaired anxiously to wait their return, proceeded along the High Street on his way to the stables in the Canongate. The Netherbow Port, through which the coach would have to pass, was now guarded by six junior privates of the town-guard, their seniors having got so drunk that the officer in command could not find anyone sober enough to take charge. After posting his men, the officer gave the key to the official civilian gatekeeper who in turn, having been kept out of his bed the two previous nights by the comings and going of volunteers, considered he was fairly entitled to a good sleep and handed it to his servant with no special instructions with regard to the opening of the gate. As the coach approached, the sentry stepped into the road, and after some altercation with the driver refused to let him pass; but the servant now appeared, said that all was in order, and the gate was opened. The coach had scarcely trundled through when the Highlanders rushed forward, charged through the still half-open gate, seized the guard and then clattered down the High Street, claymores in hand, ready to tackle anyone offering resistance. It was soon evident there were none.

So quickly had the capture of the city been accomplished that few were aware of what had happened even the following morning. It is said that a gentleman taking his usual morning walk on the ramparts noticed with some surprise a plaided Highlander sitting astride one of the newly-placed guns. 'Surely you are not one of the same troops who mounted guard here yesterday,' he exclaimed. 'Och no!' replied the Gael. 'They've been relieved.' That day the Prince rode into his capital at the head of the main body, taking care to avoid the guns of the Castle which had defiantly opened fire. He was dressed in a handsome short coat of tartan, the cross of St. Andrew was pinned to his blue silken sash, and in his bonnet was the Jacobite emblem in the form of a white knotted ribbon. As he passed through the streets on his way to set up his headquarters at Holyroodhouse, he was cheered by spectators, the bulk of whom were women. Meanwhile, his royal father was being proclaimed at Mercat

46

Holyrood House

Cross in the middle of the High Street. Here the whole street was densely packed with people, and from the windows of adjacent houses the cere-mony was watched by the ladies of Edinburgh who appeared to be the Prince's best supporters judging by the white rosettes so many of them wore in their hats or on their dresses. Most of the army had by this time moved on to encamp at Hunter's Bog in King's Park, but around the Cross was a small body of Camerons standing guard in three ranks.

The rest of the day was spent in requisitioning food, stores, weapons and clothing for the Highlanders, and among other items demanded from the city authorities were 1,000 tents, 2,000 targes and 6,000 pairs of shoes. It had been confidently expected that many recruits would join in Edinburgh, and drummers were sent round the city to beat up volunteers, offering in the Prince's name a sum of five guineas to each man who enlisted. The response seems to have been disappointing, though Murray of Broughton records that 'a good many entered the Duke of Perth's regiment'; on the other hand a party of Maclachlans

47

and Grants now arrived from the north. And, more important, of the thousand or so volunteers who had earlier been willing to defend the city only twenty-five left to join Cope's army. These included ex-provost Drummond and two students, the future divine Alexander Carlyle and the historian Home.

From Edinburgh the Prince and his army moved out to Duddingston with a view to coming to grips with the royal army approaching from the east, and at a council of war it was decided that the whole force should march at dawn the following morning to intercept Cope on his way from Haddington. Charles wanted to lead his men in the coming battle, but the chiefs would not allow him to risk his life so early in the campaign when success depended so much on his presence. He addressed the officers before the army left Duddingston, ending his spirited harangue with a flourish of his sword, and the words, 'Gentlemen, I have flung away the scabbard and with God's assistance I don't doubt of making you a free and happy people. Master Cope shall not escape us as he did in the Highlands.' When the officers in their turn passed on the Prince's message to their men assembled in Duddingston Park, the Highlanders responded by giving a comforting cheer. Then the Highland army, led by a small detachment of horsemen under Viscount Strathallan and Lord Elcho,[1] moved forward.

On their flight eastwards the dragoons had stopped near Prestonpans at Bankton House, the home of Colonel Gardiner, and nearby, in the fields between his estate and the village of Seton, the coming battle was to be fought. The student Home, watching from the top of the tower of his father's church, was the first to see the Highlanders advancing, and reported it to General Cope who hurried his men forward to give battle. Meanwhile, the Highland army, whose main body had crossed the Exe at Musselburgh and reached Pinkie House, now in its turn received reports that Cope's troops were approaching. It seemed as if the royal army were moving forward to occupy the hills to the south of Bankton House and Tranent, and Lord George Murray who was in the van, 'considering there was not time to deliberate and wait for orders', pushed forward and occupied this high ground before the enemy could do so. Later, when he had been joined by the Prince, they could see below them Cope's army lined up in the stubble of the cornfields east of Preston House and Bankton House, and commanding most effectively the coast roads from Edinburgh. It seemed at first that the Highland army might with advantage charge straight down the hill and take Cope in the flank; but, at closer quarters, it was seen that a huge bog lay between the two forces. It was while nearing Tranent that the High-

1. *Elcho had just joined and besides offering his services brought a valuable contri-bution in money.*

48

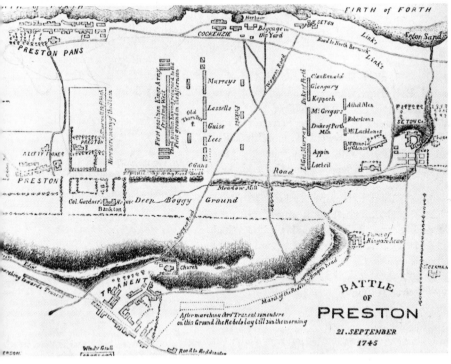

Prestonpans, from Home's History

landers were first seen by Cope's men, and Cope reacted quickly to the situation, changing the direction of his front so that it now faced the Highlanders' threatened approach from the south. On Cope's right was the twelve-foot wall of Preston House which had previously defended part of his front, and his line in the new position stretched towards Seton along the north edge of the bog.

Prince Charles shared the leadership of the Highland army with Colonel O'Sullivan, the Duke of Perth, and Lord George Murray, and it suffered from this divided control. The first move in the battle had been made by Murray in occupying the heights, but this had been done without consulting his colleagues. The Prince, unaware of this new advantage, moved a force under Lord Nairne, which included Murray's Athollmen, down to the west of Preston with the intention of threatening Cope from the direction of the coast roads and blocking his advance on Edinburgh. O'Sullivan, meanwhile, sent a small force of Camerons to occupy Tranent churchyard and watch Cope's south flank. According to O'Sullivan, this caused a deplorable scene. When Lord George heard that his brigade had been moved without his permission, he flew into a terrible rage. He threw down his pistols and declared to the Prince that

49

if his men were not immediately recalled he would resign. In the face of this outburst Charles meekly agreed, but by this time Lochiel had arrived, and he managed to pacify the irate general sufficiently for him to condescend to allow his men to remain where they were for the time being. Even so, Lord George clearly had no intention of allowing them to be ordered about without his consent. Knowing they were inadequately armed, he had already apparently refused an offer for them to occupy the right of the line, and he now no doubt considered them equally unfit for this new role. Also he probably suspected that his rival O'Sullivan was involved. Nor did the matter end quite there. He withdrew without notice the Camerons whom the quartermaster-general had placed in Tranent as soon as Lochiel reported they were being shelled and suffering casualties. This bombardment was the result of an attempt by the enemy to frighten the Highlanders. In the belief that they had never faced cannon before, Cope's men began dropping shells among them, giving a great shout at each discharge, hoping to disconcert them. O'Sullivan, who was in the rear when the order to withdraw from Tranent churchyard was issued, came up and asked what was the meaning of it; but he did accept Lord George's explanation.

The Highland army less the Atholl brigade was now halted in column in some fields of shocked peas east of Tranent, and it was at this stage that Lord George Murray began to take full charge of the conduct of the battle; the others appeared to bow to his wishes. The problem was how best to attack the enemy, and to do this it was imperative to discover whether there was any way of crossing the bog. Lord George sent Colonel Ker forward to reconnoitre. Mounted on a little grey pony, Ker went down from the hills all alone, and with great sang-froid and deliberation made a careful study of the morass from all sides, riding along unconcerned in spite of shots being fired at him from beyond the ditch along the bog's north side. He paid so little attention to the firing that when he came to a dry stone wall across his path he dismounted and coolly made a gap for himself and his pony to pass. On returning, he reported that it was quite impracticable to get at the enemy directly across the morass.

That evening a council of war was held at which Lord George Murray put forward a plan to march round the edge of the bog, cross the ditch, form up in two lines, and attack Cope's army from the east. He explained it most carefully and convinced the Prince and the other leaders, with the result that it was decided to make the rear approach early next morning. Then, after the picquets had been sent out and the Atholl brigade ordered to come in at two o'clock, the Highlanders wrapped themselves in their plaids and went to sleep on the ground; and the Prince took a sheaf of peas for a pillow and lay down in the stubble alongside them. But, during the night, a local gentleman named Robert

Anderson, whose father had been 'out' in 1715, approached one of the slumbering chiefs. He woke him, said that he had heard of their deliberations,[1] and knew of a way across the marsh. Also, if they decided to use it, he would lead them. The chief was impressed and told Anderson to wake Lord George as the suggestion would come better direct. A second council of war was promptly called and everyone agreed that Anderson's offer should be accepted.

It had been decided earlier that the previous day's order of march should be reversed so that the Macdonalds could take the right of the line. This entailed a complicated movement to bring the rear to the van, which was again entrusted to the versatile Colonel Ker. Ker went to the head of the column and told them to stand fast until he returned. Then, on reaching the rear, he ordered it to about march and pass close beside and back up the column. He repeated the order from time to time to the different clans, and thus carried through the whole manoeuvre without the least confusion. Finally, accompanied by Anderson, the Duke of Perth led the van out into the night. They headed in an easterly direction until they reached Ringanhead Farm and then turned left down a small valley and took a path across the bog selected by Anderson. They moved in complete silence, having left the horses behind at the farm in case the noise of their movement warned the enemy of their approach. The path across the bog was so narrow that it only allowed three men to march abreast, and in places so soft that they sank to their knees. Several side-tracks left the path but Anderson confidently led them straight on until they reached an unguarded wooden bridge over the bordering ditch well to the east of Cope's outposts. The front half of the column then crossed the ditch and marched forward deep into the stubble field. Led by the Macdonalds, and followed by the Macgregors, Grants, Stewarts and Camerons, they finally turned left and halted to form the front line of the Highland attack. In the meantime a body of sixty Camerons under Clanranald was despatched towards the enemy baggage train at Cockenzie with orders to seize it while the rest of the army were dealing with Cope's main body.

When the Duke of Perth's and Lord George's[2] men were all across the ditch, Chevalier Johnstone went back to bring up the rear half of the column. This included the Athollmen, the Robertsons – with Struan as a spectator – the Maclachlans and the Macdonalds of Glencoe; it was led by the Prince himself and was to form the second line in the battle. But Johnstone apparently led them down the wrong path back through

1. *Some authorities say he was actually present at the first meeting. He had been too shy to make his suggestion then, but had now thought better of it.*
2. *The Duke of Perth commanded the right and Lord George Murray the left, but the latter assumed overall command.*

the bog, for they reached the bordering ditch away from the wooden bridge. The ditch was only a few feet wide and the Prince jumped it, but fell on his knees on the far side. He was immediately helped to his feet, but looked unhappy as if he considered it a bad omen.

Dawn was now breaking and only a mist hid the two armies from each other. It was at this stage that Cope's picquets first heard the tramp of the Highlanders and realized they were being attacked. 'Who's there?' they called and, on receiving no answer, sounded the alarm. To good effect it seemed, for soon an alarm gun was heard in the distance. Cope, who was a professional soldier of experience, reacted quickly. He again changed his front so as to face the enemy, and the only confusion that occurred in a complicated manoeuvre was some bunching on the south flank where the artillery and the three squadrons of cavalry could not form up in line, and had to take up their positions one behind the other with the artillery under Colonel Whitefoord in front.

After the two lines of the Highland army had been drawn up, the Prince moved over and harangued the officers of both flanks in turn, and then took up a position in the centre of the second line surrounded by his guards. If he had been at all apprehensive when he fell at the ditch, he was now cool and self-possessed. By the time the various arrangements on both sides were completed, the sun had risen and the armies stood revealed. Cope's at this time made a formidable appearance, and some of Charles's officers were heard afterwards to declare that, when they first saw it and compared the gallant appearance of its horse and foot and their well-polished accoutrements glittering in the sun with their own badly-armed force broken in clusters, they fully expected to be defeated and driven from the field.

Everything was now in readiness. The Highlanders removed their bonnets and, placing themselves in an attitude of devotion with upraised eyes, uttered a short prayer.[1] But at the last minute Lord George Murray became concerned when he discovered that the front line had advanced too far and that Cope's right overlapped them. To rectify this he ordered the Camerons on the left of the Highland line to incline left, and directed them straight at the royal guns and Colonel Gardiner's dragoons. Indeed he was so anxious that he sent his own left flank into the attack before finding out whether the Duke of Perth's men were ready, and although he sent over an officer to ask them to make a move, the Highland left was in action long before the right.

Cope's artillery under Colonel Whitefoord had a guard of a hundred men, but only Mr. Griffiths, an old master-gunner, and a few inexperienced youths actually to serve the guns. The Camerons fired a few shots as they approached and the artillery guard replied with a sharp

1. Caledonian Mercury, *23 September, 1745.*

volley, whereupon the youths fled in a panic taking most of the powder-horns with them. Nevertheless, Colonel Whitefoord and Mr. Griffiths between them managed to fire eleven shells from the mortars and guns by loading and firing the pieces themselves. But although this caused some casualties among the Camerons it did not stop them, and a second volley from the artillery guard appeared to have no effect on the Highlanders at all. Then, seeing that the leading dragoons under Lieutenant-Colonel Whitney were about to charge, the Highlanders rushed forward with a great shout past the silent cannon, and slashed at the noses of the troopers' horses. This tactic of going for the horse before the rider proved most effective, for the maddened and uncontrollable animals turned and galloped to the rear scattering the artillery guard in their flight. The panic affected the rear squadrons too; without waiting to give battle they turned and made off after the others. Only Colonel Gardiner stayed to fight it out. Deserted by his own men, he attached himself to some foot soldiers who were attempting to defend themselves. 'Fire on, my lads,' he shouted, 'and fear nothing.' Scarcely had the words left his lips than a Cameron dealt him a terrible blow with a Lochaber axe, and a second later he was dragged from his horse and despatched by a stroke on the back of his head.

Meanwhile, the rest of the Highlanders were advancing, and the royal infantry met them with a volley fired from right to left: from Lee's, from Guise's and finally from Murray's, who were flanked by Hamilton's dragoons. Few Highlanders dropped and the survivors received the volley with a shout of defiance. Then, they abandoned their muskets, drew their broad-swords, and charged the royal infantry before they had time to reload. Confounded by the flight of the dragoons on the right, and the furious onslaught of the Highlanders, the astonished infantry threw down their arms and took to their heels and fled; and no effort on the part of their officers could make them turn round and face their adversaries. As for Hamilton's dragoons on the left, they turned and fled before Murray's had fired their volley, and without even discharging their pistols at the enemy. In their ranks and carried along with them in flight was ex-Provost Drummond, who was present on an old dragoon horse lent by a friend who had originally bought it for £4 as a cart horse. The animal was no doubt glad to get back among its fellows, but equally willing to gallop off with them in cowardly flight. Drummond had originally intended to join his friend Gardiner's regiment. But he could not reach them as the battle had started by the time he rode up, so had attached himself to Hamilton's. His friends consoled him afterwards that he was lucky to be still alive.

The attack of the Highland centre was particularly spirited and vio-lent, and, according to Johnstone, the Macgregors were outstanding. Armed with scythes fixed to poles seven feet high, they literally mowed down the enemy by cutting off their limbs. They were led by Rob Roy's son. When he fell with two bullets through him and was lying prostrate on the ground, in order that his men should not lose impetus, he rested his head on his hand and called out, 'My lads, I am not dead yet! By God, I shall see if any fail in their duty!'

The royal infantry were hampered by the walls and hedges of Preston House and Bankton House which barred their flight to the rear. Having thrown away their arms to escape more quickly, they found themselves herded up against the walls and quite unable to protect themselves. The slaughter was terrible and might have been even worse had the officers not restrained their men, and the men themselves eventually shown compassion. Nevertheless, the ruthless killing carried out by the Highlanders at Prestonpans in some way explains the fearful retribution at Culloden later, for, according to the *Caledonian Mercury* of 25 September, 'the field of battle presented an appalling spectacle rarely exhibited even in the most bloody conflicts. As almost all the slain were cut down by the broadsword and the scythe, the ground was strewn with legs, arms, hands, and mutilated bodies'.

It was a short affair. In a few minutes the whole of Cope's army was put to flight and his baggage train at Cockenzie captured. Of the 2,000 or so in the field, except for the cavalry, only about 170 escaped. The cavalry crowded back through the defiles between Bankton House and Preston House. Cope and some of his officers tried hard to make them turn and fight; but either because the horses were too ill-trained, or their riders too cowardly, the only direction in which they could be persuaded to move was away from the enemy. Finally Cope managed to assemble the bulk of them west of Prestonpans, and from there led them through Preston village, up the so-called 'Johnny Cope's Road', and away to the south to Coldstream. Eventually they reached Berwick where it was said spitefully that Cope was the only general to bring the first news of his own defeat.

The Jacobite losses by contrast were small: about forty killed and ninety wounded. Cope's baggage train had been guarded by Loudon's Highlanders, two depleted companies of the Black Watch and forty infantry of the line, but it fell to Clanranald's detachment without a fight; the guard was too dispirited by the flight of the royal army to offer any resistance. It provided rich pickings, for besides the rest of the guns there was a sum of £4,000 in the campaign chest. Cope's carriage and his spare accoutrements were presented to the veteran Struan, who was driven off in the carriage wrapped in Cope's fur-lined cloak. It is said that when the vehicle at last approached his home in the north it could not be manoeuvred along the narrow lanes, whereupon his clansmen took out the horses and carried the carriage bodily with Struan still sitting inside.

A Race from Preſton Pans to Berwick.

Cartoon of Sir John Cope who is said to have been the first general to have brought the news of his own defeat

After the battle the compassionate Prince Charles ordered his doctors to attend the wounded of both sides impartially. He took his supper on the field of battle and then repaired for the night to Pinkie House, the seat of his enemy Lord Tweeddale. From Pinkie he returned to Holyrood and his army to the camps in and around Edinburgh. The startling result of the occupation of the capital and the subsequent victory at Prestonpans was that, with the exception of the castles at Edinburgh, Stirling and Dumbarton, and a few forts in the north, the whole of Scotland was now under his control.

Prince Charles only allowed limited celebrations of his victory at Prestonpans as he could not rejoice at the death or injury of any of his father's subjects even though they had taken up arms against him. Soon after he had set up his headquarters again at Holyrood, he appointed an advisory council made up of the principal leaders. This was no doubt valuable, but the manner in which he conducted the subsequent meetings offended some of the chiefs. His old friends George Kelly, Sir Thomas Sheridan, Colonel O'Sullivan, Colonel Strickland and the veteran Sir John Macdonald, all of whom had come over on the *Du Teillay*, were willing to support without question any course the Prince wanted; but others like Lord George Murray and Lord Ogilvy often

55

E

thought they knew better than their young master, and did not mind saying so, with the result that Charles came to dislike them simply because they disagreed with him. And they for their part sneered at the so-called Irish clique[1] for being too compliant.

Since the arrival of the Highlanders in Edinburgh a tacit agreement had existed between them and the Castle garrison whereby provisions of every description, especially for the officers, were permitted to pass into the Castle. This understanding was destroyed by a series of incidents towards the end of September, and only with difficulty restored. It seems to have been disrupted initially by General Guest trying to detain the Highland army as soon as he heard it was planning to invade England. At any rate his guns and riflemen opened a desultory fire in the direction of West Port where the Highlander guards had previously allowed those carrying provisions to pass through. In retaliation all ways towards the Castle were sealed off. When Guest heard of the blockade, he sent a letter to Lord Provost Stewart saying that unless it were ended his guns would compel the Highland guards to evacuate West Port, and at the

1. Strickland was in fact English and Sir John Macdonald only Irish in that he had commanded Irish troops for the French King.

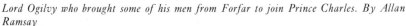

Lord Ogilvy who brought some of his men from Forfar to join Prince Charles. By Allan Ramsay

same time subject the city to bombardment. In his reply the Provost endeavoured to show that this was an unreasonable demand, as the citizens had no control over those responsible for the blockade. Guest remained inflexible, and the Provost next sent six deputies to beg for the assistance of Prince Charles. The Prince, on reviewing the matter, expressed disgust at the inhumanity of General Guest, particularly as the Castle was known to possess six weeks' provisions in hand and the lifting of the blockade was not necessary for the survival of the garrison; he said that if Guest persisted he would take reprisals on the estates of officers in the Castle and other gentlemen outside who supported the Government; but he would not lift the blockade.

This led to a minor war between the Castle and the army posts around West Port, with casualties mainly among the innocent local citizens. Guest's guns opened fire and destroyed several houses in the neighbourhood of West Port, and Prince Charles retaliated by issuing an official proclamation prohibiting contact with the garrison on pain of death, and by surrounding the Castle with armed posts. The garrison thereupon opened fire at every Highlander within range, and one of their number slipped out and set fire to a house in Livingston's yards, shot dead one of the guards, and returned safely. After this the men in the fortress grew bolder. Half-moon Battery above the castle-gate bombarded the Highlanders' posts all one afternoon and evening; and directly it was dark, and the guns had ceased, a party sallied forth and set fire to a foundry and house on Castle Hill. The garrison next came out in force and dug a trench fourteen feet broad and sixteen feet deep across the approach to the Castle, half-way between the castle-gate and the first houses on Castle Hill. Along its parapet, made from earth thrown up from the trench, 200 men were posted, and these opened fire on all and sundry who came within range, killing and wounding a number of inhabitants and Highlanders. Next day the bombardment from Half-moon Battery was resumed on an increased scale and with an even more disastrous effect on the city; no one could appear with safety in the High Street, as the shots penetrated as far down as old Fleshmarket Close. All this caused something like a panic in the west end and a number of people, mainly women and children, rushed out into the countryside taking as many of their possessions as they could carry.

The distress being caused to the civilian population caused the good-natured Prince to have second thoughts, and after a number of appeals from the town council he decided on humanitarian grounds to yield to General Guest's demand to relax the blockade. Yet in the end neither achieved his aims. The Prince's attempt to put pressure on the garrison by limiting their food supply certainly failed, but so did Guest's effort to keep the Highland army in Edinburgh, for very soon afterwards it left to invade England.

Chapter VI

CARLISLE

'The garrison of Carlisle in 1745 consisted of two companies of invalided soldiers, two companies of militia, a
troop of militia horse, and three artillerymen under
Master-Gunner Stevenson to whose care were entrusted the twenty 6-pounder cannon which were all the
town could boast of.'
Carlisle in 1745 by GEORGE G. MOUNSEY, 1846

While Charles was still at Edinburgh, news came that a ship from France
with money, arms and ammunition, and, as an ambassador from the
French court, the Marquis Boyer d'Eguille, had anchored at Montrose.
Two other vessels followed bringing more money and ammunition, six
field guns with a company of artillerymen, and a number of Irish officers
in the service of France. These were a welcome contribution, and every
effort was now made to increase the force at the Prince's disposal by
asking some chiefs, who had already joined, to return to the north and
induce their neighbours to support the cause. Meanwhile, Duncan
Forbes of Culloden was trying to persuade hesitant chiefs around Inverness to help the Government by sending men to enlist under chosen
leaders in twenty independent companies[1] of loyal Highlanders which
he had been authorized to raise. To start with, by pointing out in forcible
terms the ruin which would befall the chiefs and their families should
the Prince fail, Forbes had some success. The victory at Prestonpans,
however, made his task more difficult, just as it inevitably helped Charles
in his efforts to gain more supporters.

Among the waverers was still Lord Lovat; but some of his Fraser
clansmen, keener than their chief to follow the Stuart standard, and
exasperated at Forbes's manoeuvres, persuaded Murray of Broughton
to draw up in the Prince's name a warrant for the Lord President's
arrest and then evolved a plan to attack his home and capture him. With
this intent, a party of them approached Culloden House on 5 October
and attempted to storm their way in. Forbes, however, had been fore-
warned of the plot against him, and had not only fortified his home but
filled it with armed supporters, so that the Frasers were easily driven off.

1. See appendix.

Simon Fraser, Lord Lovat, whose main home was at Dounie, north-west of Inverness. He could not decide which side to join but ended by being executed for treason. By Simon after Le Clare

They sought compensation for their failure by stealing many of his cattle; but for the future they left him in peace; and their chief, although undoubtedly in the know, even went so far as write a long letter of condolence to the Lord President disclaiming any responsibility. Lovat, as usual finding difficulty in deciding which side to join, also eventually allowed 500 Frasers and Chisholms to march south and help the Prince, although they did not arrive in time to take part in the invasion of England.

Sir Alexander Macdonald[1] of Skye had already declared for the Government, and he persuaded Macleod of Macleod of Skye to do likewise, but some 200 from the island led by Mackinnon of Mackinnon joined the Prince in Edinburgh. Other adherents at this time were the veteran Gordon of Glenbucket and Lord Pitsligo who each arrived with several hundred men drawn from the Banff and Aberdeen areas, and

1. Usually called Sir Alexander Macdonald of Sleat.

Lord Ogilvy who joined with 600 from Angus. In addition, Colonel Roy Stewart had raised a Jacobite Edinburgh regiment of 450. But there was one disaster. Among those sent north to try to persuade laggard chiefs to bring out their clans was Kinlochmoidart at whose home Charles had stayed after landing at Loch-nan-Uamh. After a round of visits during which he received hopeful promises of support, he was passing with a single servant across a desolate moor in Lanarkshire to rejoin the Prince when he was set upon by a party of Government supporters armed with pitchforks and fowling-pieces. The servant opened fire, but when Kinlochmoidart realized that resistance was hopeless and would only result in needless bloodshed, he allowed himself to be taken prisoner. He was put at once under a strong guard and eventually taken to Carlisle where he was tried and executed with other Jacobites, for treason. It was tragic that he should be lost so early in the campaign, particularly at a time when George Kelly had been sent to France to seek further help on the strength of the victory at Prestonpans, for the very small group of Charles's most loyal supporters was sharply reduced in numbers.

Macdonald of Kinlochmoidart's stick. He was captured by Government supporters while trying to raise more men for the Prince

On the other side, Duncan Forbes managed to enroll two independent companies in the north by the end of October, though it took him several months to complete the twenty authorized. Forbes's companies were manned principally by Munroes, Grants, Sutherlanders, Mackays, Macleods and Macdonalds from Skye, Mackenzies, Rosses and some Gordons, and there was an independent company raised in Inverness. The greatest number of Highlanders raised for the Government were embodied at the instigation of the Duke of Argyll under his kinsman General Campbell and the latter's son Colonel John Campbell.[1] These two professional soldiers trained and brought into action several thousand Argyll militia – and so after all the dreaded Campbells were armed. But they did not play an active part until after the invasion of England, and their main contribution to the Government cause came

1. *General Campbell was a cousin of the 3rd Duke, and subsequently succeeded to the title. His son John eventually became the 5th Duke.*

at Culloden, during the pursuit after the battle, and in the pacification of the Highlands.

Having spent nearly six weeks in Edinburgh, the Prince now considered that he could no longer delay his intended march into England. By postponing departure he might increase his force by the addition of the troops in the process of being raised locally, and by small bodies of Highlanders from the north; but the waiting time might well be used by the Government to withdraw more men from the Continent and concentrate such an overwhelming force that they would no longer hesitate to attack – Field Marshal Wade already had a larger army[1] than the Prince's but, owing to his respect for the fighting qualities of the Highlanders after studying reports from Prestonpans, he did not feel inclined to move until reinforced. Another reason for an immediate invasion was the rate of desertion which the idle weeks in Edinburgh had brought about, and which it was felt would cease once the army was on the move; but the main inducement was the assurance that there was wide support for the Stuart cause in England. When the Prince announced to the council that he had received the strongest evidence of this, 'a unanimous resolution was entered into to march into England'.[2]

The next matter to be decided was the route they would take. After some deliberation most of the council agreed the best plan was to march on Berwick and Newcastle and join battle with Wade. If victorious, the Prince could then march on London down the east coast and be in reach of any reinforcements sent over from France. Lord George Murray was one of those who demurred. He suggested they should march due south from Edinburgh on Carlisle and invade England down the west side where there were both stronger Jacobite support and a mountainous terrain advantageous to the Highlanders. He explained his plan so convincingly that all eventually were won over to it.

On Sunday, 3 November, with all the necessary preparations now complete, the army set off in two columns, with the Duke of Perth and the baggage taking a route by Peebles and Moffat, and the Prince[3] at the head of the clan regiments going by Kelso and Jedburgh further east. At first the cavalry accompanied the Prince, but after passing through Jedburgh took a parallel route through Hawick and rejoined the Prince's column on the Esk twelve miles north of Carlisle. Charles led his column on foot, in Highland dress with his targe slung over his shoulder, and he won much respect throughout the army by his example. In order to allow the column with the baggage to keep pace, he stopped two days

1. *He may not have realized this.*
2. *Kirkconnel M.S.*
3. *Lord George Murray went with the Prince.*

General Campbell, who raised the Campbells for the Government and pacified the Highlands after Culloden, shown in his robes as the 4th Duke of Argyll. By Gainsborough

Colonel John Campbell, son of General Campbell, who led the Campbell militia at Falkirk and commanded Lord Loudoun's 64th Regiment. He became 5th Duke of Argyll. Engraving by Heath

at Kelso, and had time to plant a rosebush, offshoots of which, called 'Prince Charlie's White Rose', are said to survive in some gardens there. On 9 November the two columns combined on English soil and approached Carlisle.

At the news of the Highlanders' invasion, and the threat to Carlisle,

General Wade, who in an attempt to pacify the Highlands raised the Black Watch and built roads and bridges to expedite the movement of troops

the Government appointed Colonel Durand to organize the defence of the city. This was a difficult task as the garrison consisted of only a few invalided soldiers and some militia, and no reinforcements were offered. Although there were nominally both a Governor of the Castle and a Mayor, neither played a leading role in the defence arrangements, and Colonel Durand had to rely for support on the Deputy-Mayor Pattinson and Dr. Waugh from the cathedral. Waugh had heard earlier that the Highlanders were likely to assault the city, and had despatched a letter containing the news to the Duke of Newcastle. He was most cooperative throughout. Pattinson was initially bold, declaring that he would rather die than surrender, but his resolve weakened as the danger grew.

The militia horse out on reconnaissance to the north were the first to report the Highlanders' approach, but soon they were sighted by Dr.

Waugh and some of the clergy who were keeping watch from the tower of the cathedral, using 'a very large spying glass' which Durand had brought. The clerics noticed the enemy near Grimber Hill two miles north of the city, and an hour later at Stanwix, just across the Eden from Carlisle, where the river runs for a short distance in two channels. Shortly afterwards a local farmer arrived with a letter from Colonel O'Sullivan demanding quarters in Carlisle for 13,000 foot and 300 horse. These exaggerated demands were always made by Charles's quartermasters in order to deceive the Government about the size of his army. It proved an effective hoax, for Wade was convinced the Highland army was as big or bigger than his own, and when the Prince was marching through Lancashire it was reported in England that he had 7,000 with him instead of 4,000. No reply was made to the demand for quarters and, to show their defiance, the castle guns prepared to open fire; but it was market day, and a number of country people were going home through Stanwix, and became mixed up with the Highlanders, so 'it was impossible for the garrison to fire upon them for some time without risk of injuring their neighbours along with their enemies. But in less than half an hour, the country people dispersed themselves, when the garrison of the castle fired a ten-gun battery upon them, which it is believed killed several. Certainly, at night they retreated to a greater distance from the city'.[1]

On Sunday, 10 November a formal demand in writing was received from Charles for the surrender of the town within two hours. The letter proclaimed his father's rights, and promised the citizens protection if they complied with his wishes; but threatened the town with force, and all its consequences, if they refused. Regardless of this threat, the leaders decided that no answer should be sent, and the messenger, another innocent farmer forced to do the job, was detained. The result was that the Prince, true to his word, started siege operations forthwith. Colonel Durand, meanwhile, sent off an express to Field Marshal Wade saying that if he did not send help the town was likely to fall.

By the time Charles ordered the investment of Carlisle, his whole army had crossed the Eden to the west of the town. Lord George Murray was offered command of the operation, but because of his lack of experience in siege warfare decided to undertake the posting of the beleaguering troops and leave the emplacement and employment of the batteries to the Duke of Perth who had conducted sieges on the Continent. By doing this Lord George offended the Prince who from then on sent all orders directly to the Duke of Perth, implying that Lord George no longer enjoyed overall command of the operations.

The day was dark and gloomy, and a dense November fog hung over

1. *Based on an eye-witness account in* Transactions in Scotland.

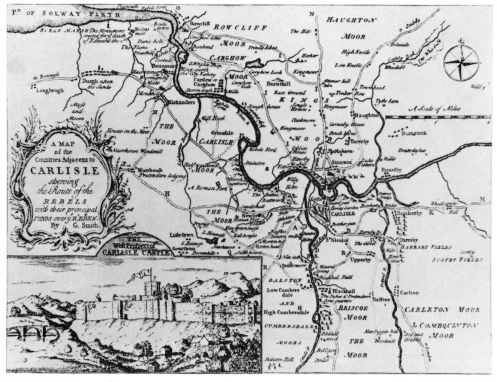

Carlisle by G. Smith

the country, screening the movements of both sides. The Duke of Perth, Colonel O'Sullivan, and an Irish officer of Lally's Regiment who had recently arrived at Montrose from France and was an experienced engineer, boldly rode up to within pistol shot of the walls and selected a site for the batteries near the Penrith road north-west of the town. There were available for emplacement the six Swedish field pieces recently arrived from France and the seven guns captured from Cope at Prestonpans. The Duke of Perth's men provided the detachment to dig the trenches and to guard them; but as they were also expected to make the assault, they started by cutting wood in Corby and Warwick parks to provide fascines and scaling ladders. When dusk fell, they began digging; but had not accomplished much before the order to invest was cancelled and they were marched away. That night, when Charles had returned to his quarters in the village of Black Hall[1] south of the town,

1. *The Duke of Perth was at Stanwix north of the town and Lord George Murray at Harraby about the same distance to the east.*

a special messenger brought news that Field Marshal Wade was coming to relieve the town. Anxious to remove the threat from Newcastle once and for all, Charles gave orders for the whole army to quit the siege and move out to Brampton, a small village seven miles north-east of Carlisle on the Newcastle road where hilly country provided good defensive positions.

The withdrawal led the inhabitants of Carlisle to conclude that the siege had been abandoned, and they began to congratulate themselves on their lucky escape. Pattinson was particularly pleased, and wrote off to Lord Lonsdale, the Lord Lieutenant, sending a copy of the Prince's demand for the surrender of the city, and adding, 'that he had returned no answer thereto but by firing the cannon upon them, and that their whole army was at the time of despatching the above advice marched to Brampton, seven miles on the high road to Newcastle'.[1] The satisfaction of the citizens, however, was short-lived. As soon as the army reached Brampton, news was received that it was all a false alarm and Wade was not on the way, so the two contingents under the Duke of Perth and Lord George Murray were sent back to resume the siege operations, and trenches and emplacements were immediately dug 300 yards away from the Castle and town between the Scots and English gates.

Neither the task of standing guard, nor that of digging the emplacements and trenches was agreeable to the Duke of Perth's men and it was only with great difficulty that he kept them at it in the very cold weather; but both he and Tullibardine who was assisting took off their coats and worked alongside their soldiers to set an example, and eventually the job was done to everyone's satisfaction. Lord George Murray called for volunteers from the Atholl brigade to help with guard duties in the trenches; but these men did not particularly appreciate the thought of standing about in the cold either, and they said they would only undertake it for twenty-four hours, and then only if the six battalions still at Brampton took their turn. Murray worked out a complicated system of reliefs which included the employment of the Brampton half of the army, and put the plan before the Prince's council of war; but the council turned it down because they did not think it fair to employ the Brampton battalions, 'as they had had all the fatigue and danger of the blockade in Edinburgh'.

Just at the very moment when the Highland army recommenced siege operations Colonel Durand received the long-awaited reply to his letter asking for help from Field Marshal Wade; and it was far from encouraging, for it made it clear to everyone concerned in the defence of the city that nothing was to be expected from him. The roads, Wade

1. Caledonian Mercury.

wrote, were impassable for artillery; there would be no provisions for the men after the Highlanders had 'ravaged and consumed what they find in their way'; and as Lancashire seemed the destination of the invaders, Carlisle would probably be left unmolested; he hoped, however, to meet the rebels later in Lancashire and 'cause them to repent their rashness'. Wade's disappointing answer coupled with the reappearance of the Highland army caused a serious decline of morale in the city. A group of militia notified Colonel Durand that they could not control their men and asked to be allowed to retire with their companies by the English gate. Durand was indignant and refused point-blank to open the gate. At last, following appeals to their honour by their colonel and Dr. Waugh, the militia agreed to resume duty and guard the walls for another night. All was well until morning when the sight of the enemy guns in their emplacements caused a further loss of courage, and another appeal to Colonel Durand to let them depart. Durand decided to inspect the guns himself, to find out how menacing they really were. After viewing them from the ramparts, he came to the conclusion that they were too small to do much harm. However, on repairing to the King's Arms to report his findings to the militiamen he found that the craven crowd had already decided to capitulate.

The inhabitants at this juncture had come to no decision, but during the day a meeting was held in the Town Hall to discuss the matter. Pattinson was in the chair and immediately put to the meeting the question: 'Shall we open the gate to the rebels, or not open the gates?' Dr. Waugh and several other prominent townspeople did not approve of the form of this question, as it gave only two alternatives. They suggested a different wording which offered a third choice, namely that they should let the militia capitulate, but themselves repair to the Castle. The meeting became noisy, with no prospect of anything being decided, so Dr. Waugh and his supporters left. Later, when they called on Colonel Durand in the Castle, they found with him a number of officers and others from the invalid companies and the militia who were willing to continue to hold out; and they all set about transporting weapons, ammunition and food into the citadel to make it secure for a prolonged siege.

Meanwhile, Pattinson's courage had quite evaporated, and he and the less staunch citizens who had remained behind in the Town Hall decided to seek the best terms they could obtain from the Prince. With this in view they caused a white flag to be displayed on the city walls, and empowered the real Mayor, who had at last come out of his seclusion, to seek terms on their behalf. Charles was quietly enjoying his supper in his quarters at Brampton when the news came that the white flag had been seen on the walls and the city was prepared to capitulate. It seemed too good to be true, but he sent Murray of Broughton to the

Duke of Perth's camp at Stanwix to investigate, and if possible to join with Perth in arranging the terms of surrender. The Mayor and three deputies were already with the Duke when Murray of Broughton arrived. They agreed to give up the town provided the liberties and effects of the townspeople were not interfered with, and the militia were allowed to retire to their homes in the countryside. They promised that all the cannon and other arms would be surrendered in the condition they were in when the white flag was raised. As far as the Castle was concerned they could say nothing: they explained that Colonel Durand was obdurate and was determined not to yield; they hoped, however, that the Prince would not make the city suffer on that account.

The Duke of Perth and Murray of Broughton did not feel able to decide the matter of the Castle holding out, and referred the citizens' offer to the Prince. Next morning his answer arrived. It read: 'He would grant no terms to the Town, nor treat about it at all unless the Castle was surrendered; but if that were done all would receive honourable terms: the inhabitants would be protected in their persons and estates, and everyone would be at liberty to go where he pleased.' As the Mayor had no authority to speak on behalf of Colonel Durand or the other officers and gentlemen who were with him in the Castle, he still pleaded his inability to do more than he had already promised; but the Duke of Perth and Murray of Broughton, supported by the Prince's letter, would consent to nothing but a complete surrender of the town and Castle, and threatened that unless the Prince's instructions were met they would open fire at once and compel submission. This settled the matter, and the Mayor having agreed to try to arrange for the capitulation of the whole garrison departed with his deputies to lay the matter before Durand. When they reached the city, and the result of their mission became known, the inhabitants clamoured for instant surrender fearing that otherwise the bombardment would begin. When approached, Durand, having heard the noise in the town and been told the cause, conferred with his fellow officers in the Castle and, finding that the majority had changed their view once again and now felt it would be foolish and inhumane to hold out any longer, he reluctantly added his signature to the surrender document which had been drawn up.

Now that terms had been settled, the Duke of Perth with his division entered Carlisle by the English gate and took possession of the city and Castle. Next morning, attended by the Mayor and civic officials in their robes, he proclaimed King James with due ceremony at the Market Cross, and later in the day the Mayor and Corporation rode out to Brampton and presented the keys of the city to the Prince, kneeling at his feet in token of submission.

There were only two casualties during the siege, and both on the Prince's side. One man in the trenches was wounded, and a newly arrived

Highmoor House, Carlisle

Irish officer who was standing up taunting his men that they were not doing as well as the town's officers was hit in the throat by a cannon ball and killed. The tangible spoils were the cannon and military stores, 1,000 stand of arms and 200 good horses. Also, the easy capture of an English fortified town following so close on the victory at Prestonpans caused considerable alarm in the minds of many English people, and raised morale in the Highland army sufficiently for Prince Charles to persuade the men to follow him away from their homes deep into English territory.

This first success on English soil was, however, marred by dissension among the leaders. Lord George Murray angered the Prince by rejecting his offer to command the siege operations, and in return Lord George was offended because thereafter the Prince dealt only with the Duke of Perth, and ignored him in the transmission of orders. Also the Prince had appointed the Duke of Perth and Murray of Broughton to arrange the terms of surrender for the city. Lord George considered the Duke as a Roman Catholic unsuitable to have direct dealings in such matters with the English, and was jealous of Murray of Broughton whom he looked upon as a rival and whose views he despised. The snub which provided the final straw, however, was the refusal by the council to adopt his method of supplying reliefs for those digging, guarding and manning the emplacements; and this was the complaint he stressed in his letter of resignation.[1]

'Sir, – I cannot but observe how little my advice as a general officer has any weight with your Royal Highness, ever since I had the honour of a commission from your hands. But as I ever had a firm attachment to the royal family, and in particular to the king, my master, I shall go on as a volunteer, and design to be this night in the trenches as such, with any other that will please to follow me, though I own I think there are full few on this post already. Your Royal Highness will please order whom you think fit to command on this post and the other parts of the blockade. I have the honour to be, Sir, your Royal Highness's most faithful and most humble servant.

(signed) George Murray

Lord Elcho has command till you please appoint it otherwise.

This letter greatly upset the Prince, as, though he was already beginning to dislike his senior lieutenant-general, he realized his ability as a commander and the seriousness of the loss of his services. He replied, however, with his usual dignity:

Brampton. 14 Nov. 1745

'I think your advice ever since you joined me at Perth has had another guess weight with me than that what any general officer could claim as such. I am therefore extremely surprised you should throw up your commission for a reason which I believe was never heard of before. I am glad of your particular attachment to the King, but I am very sure he will never take anything as a proof of it but your deference to me. I accept your demission as lieutenant-general and your future services as a volunteer.

Charles P.R.[2]

Lord George Murray's letter caused great indignation among the Prince's intimates. Sir John Macdonald, no admirer of the touchy general, called it impertinent; and he and Colonel Strickland considered it a good opportunity of getting rid of a man they sometimes suspected of treachery. Colonel O'Sullivan agreed, and, no doubt because of the Prestonpans incidents, would not even concede that he was a good general. The Duke of Perth and Murray of Broughton, however, took a different view. Believing the Prince's interests were all that mattered,

1. *Chambers.*
2. *Atholl Chronicles.*

they both took steps to help settle the trouble. Murray of Broughton said that 'rather than Lord George should resign on his account he requested the Prince to allow him to absent himself from the council of war, which Charles after some protestations permitted him to do, which seemed to quiet Lord George a good deal'.[1] The Duke of Perth went even further. Although he denied strongly that because he was a Roman Catholic it was improper for him to hold a command in England, nevertheless, as he had nothing at heart but the Prince's interest, he offered his resignation: and to add to his magnanimity, offered with his men to take charge of the baggage when the army marched, as Lord Ogilvy had threatened to throw up his commission and serve as a volunteer rather than that his Angus men should be employed in such work.[2] The generous behaviour of Perth and Broughton led to the reinstatement of both generals during the stay in Carlisle, and the matter was settled for the time being.

The following days were occupied in taking over the military stores lodged in the Castle and making arrangements for the next move. A council of war was held on 18 November at which four plans were discussed. First, to march towards Newcastle and engage Field Marshal Wade; second, to return to Scotland and carry on a defensive war until the army was strong enough to take the offensive; third, to remain at Carlisle and await a general rising of the English Jacobites; and fourth, to continue the march south to Lancashire where a considerable accession of King James's supporters might be looked for. The last suggestion commended itself to the Prince, and, after it had been agreed by the others, he immediately expressed his intention of acting upon it.

1. *Memorials of John Murray of Broughton.*
2. *Letter of Lord Ogilvy to Lady Ogilvy.*

Chapter VII

DERBY

'His Royal Highness's army did not lose more than forty men in the expedition including the twelve at Clifton. Upon the whole never was a march performed with more cheerfulness and executed with greater vigour and resolution which next to the visible protection of Almighty God was owing the example shown by his Royal Highness who always marched on foot at the head of his men.'

JACOBITE RELICS

Lord Strathallan had been left at Perth to assemble new recruits, and before leaving Carlisle Charles sent a messenger north to direct him to lead them down into England. Charles also left a garrison of 150 men at Carlisle, and ordered Lord Kilmarnock with his horse to remain at Brampton to watch Wade's movements. Then, the first division of mixed clans under Lord George Murray, preceded by Lord Elcho's life guards handsomely uniformed in red and blue and 150 gentlemen on horseback under Lord Pitsligo, left Carlisle by the Penrith road. The second division of clan regiments led by the Prince in person followed at one day's march; but this interval was later decreased to half a day. Numerous camp followers including a number of prostitutes went with the army, and some wives accompanied their husbands, the most noteworthy being Lady Ogilvy and Mrs. Murray of Broughton.

At Penrith, Charles received a message from the cavalry left at Brampton that Wade had advanced to Hexham, and he therefore waited in case he might have to return to Carlisle and defend the city. Next day, however, he heard that Wade had retreated, and he resumed the march, though not without misgivings concerning the old general's intentions. It was learnt later that bad roads and wintry conditions had caused Wade to turn back. He suffered hundreds of casualties from exposure on the Hexham venture, and afterwards was only prepared to use his horse until conditions improved.

Before his arrival at Preston on the evening of 26 November the Prince's progress through England brought little response from the people. Their attitude was one of stolid indifference: they came out of their houses to watch the Highlanders pass, or peered at them from behind their windows as they would have at any other novel sight which

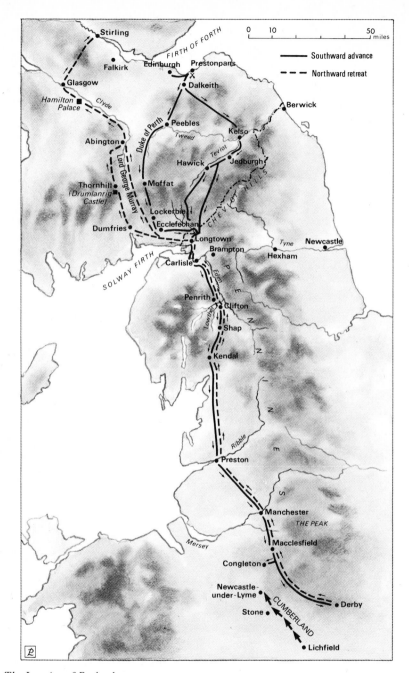

The Invasion of England

came their way, but they made no demonstration hostile or otherwise, and if there were any Jacobites among them they did not declare themselves. At Preston things were better. People crowded the pavements to cheer, and welcoming bells were heard ringing from the church steeples. Charles was joined at Preston by Mr. Francis Townley of Townley Hall, Lancashire, two Welsh gentlemen, and 'a few of the common people'. Townley was a Catholic who had served with distinction in Spain and had already been granted a commission by James.

From Preston they proceeded to Wigan and then on to Manchester where it was believed they would find many supporters. At Manchester their way was prepared for them in a most surprising fashion. Chevalier Johnstone, having found his duties as an ADC over-burdensome, had now become a company commander under the Duke of Perth, and he had acquired as his servant and company sergeant a man called Dickson who had been taken prisoner at Prestonpans and opted to serve the enemy rather than go into captivity. At Preston, Sergeant Dickson approached his master and said that he had been beating up for recruits all day without success and was upset because some of the other sergeants had done better. He asked permission to get a day's march ahead by setting out immediately for Manchester in order to make sure of some recruits before the arrival of the army. Johnstone considered it a harebrained scheme. He warned him he would probably be taken and hanged, and sent him back to his company. That evening, on returning to his quarters, his landlady told him that Dickson had gone off with his portmanteau and a blunderbuss, and Johnstone came to the conclusion the man must have left for Manchester after all.

Sergeant Dickson was accompanied by his mistress and a company drummer, and riding through the night, covered the twenty miles by morning. He immediately started to beat up for recruits for 'the yellow-haired laddie', and the people thinking the Highland army could not be far behind left him alone. However, when it came to be realized that the Highlanders were not likely to arrive before evening, the mood changed, and a mob surrounded the three of them and attempted to take them prisoner. Dickson presented his blunderbuss which was charged with slugs, and said he would blow out the brains of anyone who dared to come near. He forced his attackers to fall back by covering every direction in turn. Then, just in time, a band of Jacobites appeared who gave the necessary protection and allowed Dickson to beat up for recruits unmolested; with the result that for the expenditure of only three guineas they enrolled 180 men. Chevalier Johnstone on reaching Manchester was naturally delighted; but in the end he gained nothing from his sergeant's efforts, for the Prince decided that the volunteers should be added to a hundred or so others enrolled in the city, and formed into a Manchester regiment under the command of Francis Townley, now made a colonel. The regiment was not provided with any uniform, but Townley wore a distinctive tartan sash and the men put the white cockade of the Stuarts in their hats.

Soon after leaving Manchester, as he stepped ashore on the far side of the Mersey, Charles was greeted by a party of Cheshire gentlemen accompanied by Mrs. Skyring, an old lady whose father had fought for the Stuarts in the Cromwellian wars. Since 1660, when she had watched as a child the landing of Charles II at Dover, she had remained intensely loyal to the dynasty, and on their downfall had each year put aside money to despatch over the Channel to James II and his son. Now that James's grandson had unexpectedly arrived in Cheshire she had sold her jewels and plate and put the money in a purse to present to him. When she handed over the purse she exclaimed thankfully, 'Lord now let thy servant depart in peace;' but this proved inappropriate, for soon afterwards she heard of the Highland army's retreat and, her hopes of an early restoration quite dispelled, she dropped dead of shock.

From Manchester Charles proceeded to Macclesfield where he received news that the Duke of Cumberland had taken over command of the royal army from Ligonier, who was ill, and with 12,000 men was marching north to intercept him.

By the time the Prince's army reached Macclesfield some of the chiefs were beginning to doubt the wisdom of continuing the march into England because of the poor response; but Lord George Murray believed it would be best for them to go as far as Derby before reaching a decision, while Charles, who had not been told of the murmurings among his leaders, remained completely confident that his small army of some 5,000 could not only reach London, but turn the Hanoverian king off the throne.

On the news of the approach of Cumberland, and Wade's pursuit through Yorkshire, Lord George Murray sent a part of the Highland army westwards towards Congleton, effectively confusing the issue; Cumberland believed that the whole army was making for Wales, and promptly ordered his men north-west from Lichfield towards Stone and Newcastle-under-Lyme, thus successfully opening the way to Derby for the Highlanders who entered that city on 4 December. Led by the Prince, they marched in, in fair order, six abreast, carrying their colours, and with their pipes playing. But observers do not appear to have been much impressed. A journalist wrote in the *Derby Mercury* of 12 December: 'They were dressed in dirty plaids and as dirty shirts, without breeches and some without shoes. They really commanded our pity rather than our fear.' The officers and leaders were quartered in the homes of the local gentry, sometimes several to one house. According to the same writer from the *Derby Mercury*, the Highlanders were

Exeter House, Derby

treated to a supper of bread, cheese and beer, and those without beds were provided with plenty of straw on which to sleep in the outhouses.

At Derby, after further murmurings about the inadvisability of continuing, a council of war was called. Every day's march through England had been long, with few rest days, and recently there had been little opportunity for general discussion. As Lord George Murray wrote: 'Being fatigued they were very glad to get to their quarters; and taking care of their men with other necessities had taken up all their time.' But the two days at Derby at last offered an opportunity to debate the situation. The fateful meeting took place on 5 December, at Exeter House where the Prince had his headquarters, and most of the leaders except Sir John Macdonald were present, though Tullibardine arrived late and Murray of Broughton, who had been barred from meetings since the siege of Carlisle, was only there by chance. There was a general feeling that, with no French landing and little English support, a force of 5,000 was too small to match the 12,000 under Cumberland in front and the 9,000 under Wade behind, even without taking into consideration a third force being assembled at Finchley.

The Prince, who opened, asked for views on who should take the lead when the march was resumed, but only the Macdonalds showed much concern; and this was not in any case the topic the meeting wanted

77

Soldiers at Finchley who were moved north to protect London in 1745. By William Hogarth

to discuss, as Lord George Murray asserted when he could make his contribution, stating bluntly that he believed 'the first thing to be spoken of was how far it was prudent to advance further'. The Prince, aghast, turned towards the others, fully believing they would show themselves as shocked as he was at the suggestion of retreat; but to his amazement found they were nodding their approval. Sensing a general uneasiness, Lord George Murray begged leave to give an appreciation of the situation as he saw it and the likely results of continuing on towards London. He said he wanted a happy restoration as much as any man in Britain, and was ready to give his life and possessions to achieve it when possible. Although they were at present in a dangerous position he did not believe it was desperate. On the other hand, he felt sure that if they pressed on, the Prince would sacrifice his own life as would the bulk of the officers and men of his army. Even if they defeated the Duke of Cumberland's army in front of them, which they very well might in view of their achievements at Prestonpans, the remnants would fall back and consolidate on the Finchley force, and they would face a more formidable task with an army depleted by the losses from the first engagement. Nor was that the

78

5. THE DUKE OF CUMBERLAND.
After Sir Joshua Reynolds

complete picture, for there was still Wade's army coming down to surround them, and 'either kill or take everyone prisoner'. The chances of English Jacobites joining, already shown to be slight, must be even less likely if they were seen to have involved themselves in an impossible situation and to be facing defeat. A safe and honourable retreat was the answer: 'a successful retreat was often preferable to a victory, for the one is the effect of skill and the other often of mere chance; for his part he did not pretend to much skill, but if His Royal Highness would trust him with the management he could venture to assure him to bring the army safe back to Carlisle by the very same road they came', for the Highlanders could outmarch Cumberland's men, and as for Wade's, they had difficult country to pass and were reported to be already fatigued and sickly.

This appreciation, so cogently expressed, was received with satisfaction and applause by almost all; but the Prince, who had listened to it with ill-concealed impatience, now rose and hotly disputed Murray's arguments. Right and justice were both on his side, he said, and would undoubtedly prevail; for his personal safety he had no regard; he placed his trust in God who had hitherto protected him; but in any case death was better than disgrace. 'Rather than go back,' he passionately exclaimed, 'I would wish to be dead and buried twenty feet underground.' There was still a possibility, he continued, that French troops might effect a landing on the English coast; it was too early to assume there would be no more English assistance; many friends might yet rally round his standard before London was reached, and if these things did not materialize then they must rely upon the very audacity of their enterprise to carry them through.

At this critical moment Charles discovered to his acute disappointment that his powers of persuasion were of no avail, and his wishes were about to be entirely disregarded. Only the chivalrous Duke of Perth could be found to support him, and then through loyalty rather than conviction. Charles continued to try to make his officers change their minds, and, when he was finally convinced of the impossibility, suggested turning back to Wales rather than to Scotland, because, he said, of favourable reports from the two Welsh gentlemen who had joined them at Preston. But this plan too was rejected.

Just then, Murray of Broughton accidentally entered the conference room. He apologized, and made as if to withdraw, but the Prince called him back, telling him, with some heat, that he was quite scandalized, for everyone except the Duke of Perth was pressing him to go back to Scotland. As Murray had been barred from attending meetings and was only present by chance he had no need to give his view before the assembled group but, in spite of this, the Prince was hurt because his secretary did not openly support him. Murray justified his action by saying that, because all the leaders were against advancing, it was obviously useless to recommend it. Sir Thomas Sheridan and Colonel O'Sullivan when subsequently tackled by the Prince for remaining silent adopted the same argument.

Shortly afterwards, that most loyal of loyal supporters, Tullibardine, joined the meeting. Like the Duke of Perth he was at first inclined to support the Prince but, after listening to a summary of Lord George Murray's arguments, he too agreed that under the circumstances it would be best to return to Scotland. This was the last blow which shattered any lingering hope Charles might have had of being able to carry out his intention; all was now over, and there was nothing left for the disappointed Prince to do but consent. In a few bitter words he gave his sanction to the proposed retreat, adding by way of conclusion, 'In future I shall summon no more councils. Since I am accountable to nobody but to God and my father I shall no longer either ask or accept advice.'

Although the session was a secret one, the news of what had occurred soon leaked out, and while Lord George Murray, Cameron of Lochiel and Macdonell of Keppoch were continuing the discussion in a smaller room at Exeter House, Sir John Macdonald burst in exclaiming: 'What is this? You are going to fly without seeing the enemy? Is a Macdonald going to burn his back? Is a Cameron? Why don't you let me lead you? It is absurd to think of making such a long retreat with an undisciplined army like ours in the face of regular troops in their own country. It would be far better to take the risk and push on.' To which Lochiel replied with his customary gentleness, 'If you knew all the circumstances you would agree with us.' But Sir John was too angry to stop and listen to explanations, and he left the room. Lord George Murray explained Sir John Macdonald's attitude by saying he was old and had dined too heartily; he was very fond of the bottle and preferred campaigning in England than in Scotland because of the better amenities; also he did not fear being taken prisoner, for being nominally in the French service, he was unlikely to be condemned to death. This was probably unfair, for to give Sir John his due he was both very loyal and very brave.

It was realized that the order to retreat would be unpopular with the Highland army, for many of the men were at that moment preparing eagerly for the coming fight and having their weapons ground. In the event, though, the junior officers were not wholly displeased, for the thought of returning home was a compensation. Even the men at first were less than disgruntled, for they were given to believe that the army had turned to fight Wade's men. Nevertheless the spirit of the Highlanders was not the same during the retreat as it had been in the invasion, and their behaviour deteriorated.

The important responsibility of commanding the rearguard was assigned to Lord George Murray, and early on 6 December the retreat began. To simplify billeting arrangements the same route was followed as during the advance; but the Highlanders' reception at the towns they passed was very different. At Manchester the van was openly threatened by an angry mob, and because of these insults the Prince inflicted a fine of £5,000 on the town. He proposed, too, staying an extra day to show his defiance both to the populace and to Cumberland who was slowly pursuing him; but Lord George Murray, anxious not to waste time unnecessarily, persuaded him to allow the march to continue. As they set off there was further trouble from the crowd, and one man attempted to shoot the Prince as he rode by. However, the would-be assassin was not a close observer or a good shot, for he mistook Colonel O'Sullivan for the Prince, and missed. But this unfriendly behaviour caused the Highlanders to act very roughly in all the places they now passed through: they began stealing anything they thought would be useful, especially horses so that they could ride back home.

After a day of rest, they pushed through Preston to Lancaster, where there were several developments. Wade's cavalry were reported approaching from Yorkshire, and Charles, refusing to let it appear that his army was on the run, ordered Lord George Murray and Colonel O'Sullivan to reconnoitre a battlefield where they could stand and fight. For once, Murray was willing to countenance a delay – and collaborate with his rival – and they selected a favourable position; but the Prince changed his mind and ordered the march to continue. During the reconnaissance, two of Wade's troopers were captured, and reported that the cavalry had joined Cumberland's army at Preston.

The Prince now decided to send the Duke of Perth to fetch Lord Strathallan and his men from Perth. The Duke set off with a bodyguard of a hundred horsemen, and Lady Ogilvy and Mrs. Murray of Broughton took the opportunity to return home with him. They passed through Burton and followed the road already taken on the advance to Kendal. Before their arrival, the Mayor had received false information that the Highland army had been defeated and was in full flight, and when cavalry appeared riding hard towards the town and accompanied by two ladies in a carriage, one was assumed to be the Prince in disguise and the other his accredited mistress Jenny Cameron. Perth's horsemen entered the town, and were passing quietly through when at the Fish-market a large mob armed with clubs and stones set on them. The escort opened fire and, having cleared a passage, the carriages drove on to the bridge out of the town, where they found another crowd who started to throw stones. Again the escort cleared a way, and this time they were able to escape north on the Penrith road, although they left the Duke of Perth's servant and three others as prisoners of the mob. They ascended Shap Fell without incident but, as they were approaching Clifton on the outskirts of Penrith, they were stopped by fire by militiamen and farm labourers lining the hedgerows on either side of the road; at the same time they noticed a flaming beacon near Penrith which they learnt later had been lit to raise the countryside.

If the Duke of Perth had not been accompanied by the ladies, he would probably have cut his way through; but, from concern for their safety, he decided to go back. Short of Clifton he turned off the main route towards Cliburn three miles east, and proceeded through Culgaith and Kirby Thorpe to Newby; and then crossed the main route over to the Lake District side to Rosgill. By this time they were being pursued by a party of mounted countrymen, and at Rosgill the Duke ordered his men to face round and fire a volley. This caught the pursuers by surprise and was sufficient to disperse them.

After Rosgill they crossed back over the main route and went on to Orton. Here, twelve miles north-east of Kendal, and at last left in peace, they refreshed themselves and their horses. The Duke of Perth, never very robust, was by this time so ill that he needed a rest of two hours. Even then, he suffered a relapse and had to be left for the night; but the remainder rejoined the Highland army at Kendal on 15 December. Lord George Murray wrote: 'We got to Kendal next night; it was late before the rear got in; here we found the Duke of Perth had been obliged to return, having been attacked by the county militia.'

Next day, on the way from Kendal to Penrith, the route up Shap Fell proved difficult for the baggage train. Lord George Murray had asked to be left free of it, but the train had dropped back, and it had become his responsibility. Now he managed to acquire a number of light carts, more suitable than the heavy four-wheeled wagons to make the ascent, and transferred the ammunition to them. He considered leaving behind some of the heavier material, but received firm orders from the Prince that nothing was to be left, 'not so much as a cannon ball'. At one stage Lord George carried out this instruction to the letter. It was difficult to get the carts through the streams across the route, and it sometimes took two horses and many men to haul them over one at a time. But the Manchester regiment and the Glengarrymen proved helpful. The Manchester officers worked cheerfully up to their waists in water helping the carts across; and when a cart broke down and scattered its cannon balls the Glengarries for sixpence a ball carried them up Shap in their plaids.

On the 17th, enemy cavalry were noticed hovering behind on the way from Shap to Penrith, and at one time a party of mounted militia came between the rearguard and the main body and blocked the path; but they soon dispersed when the Glengarrymen threw down their plaids and charged. When the rearguard finally reached Clifton, Lord George Murray sent the cannon and ammunition carts with their Manchester

82

guard over Lowther River Bridge to Penrith, and remained behind to chase up some more enemy horsemen seen in the fields around Lowther Hall and Clifton village. He kept with him Colonel Roy Stewart's Edinburgh regiment, and the Glengarries. The Highlanders managed to corner two enemy in the park of Lowther Hall, and were told that Cumberland was not far behind with 4,000 horse. Lord George promptly sent Stewart to the Prince to ask for reinforcements, but although the Colonel made a strong plea, Charles believing the enemy to be only militia, refused to send any help, and instead ordered Murray and the rearguard to join the main body at Penrith. Before these instructions were delivered, however, a horseman galloped into Penrith crying out that if the rearguard were not reinforced it would be cut to pieces, and the Macphersons leapt up and hurried back to Clifton, closely followed by the Appin Stewarts.

On receiving the Prince's order to join the main body, which he realized was given without knowledge of the true situation, Lord George Murray conferred with the other officers, and deciding to disregard it, prepared for battle. Meanwhile, Cumberland's horsemen approached up the main road, and formed up on south edge of Clifton Moor facing the village. His cavalry force consisted of Bland's (3rd), Cobham's (10th) and Kerr's (11th) and detachments from these regiments were dismounted and ordered to drive the Highlanders from their positions along the hedges on either side of the road at the far end of Clifton Moor. Cobham's and Kerr's engaged the Glengarrymen and Roy Stewart's regiment at the park wall on the west of the road, and the Appin Stewarts lining hedges in front of the church; while Bland's on their far right encountered the Macphersons manning the borders of the enclosures round Clifton farm.

Bland's played the major part in the skirmish that followed, an affray which was the last battle fought on English soil. Bearing to the right, and boldly led by Colonel Honywood, they crossed the ditch at the edge of the moor and lined a hedge on the far side within musket shot of Cluny's Macphersons along another hedge by the farm. It was nearly dark by the time the two sides engaged, but the moon shone fitfully from a cloudy sky greatly to the advantage of the Highlanders whose dark clothing made them less conspicuous than the dragoons. After exchanging fire for some time in the semi-darkness by aiming at musket flashes, Cobham's and Kerr's withdrew, but Bland's still remained in position on the east edge of the moor. Lord George Murray was with Cluny's Macphersons as they crept forward towards the dragoons and, when a transient gleam of moonlight showed only a straggly hedge separating them, he ordered Cluny to charge. The Highlanders broke through the hedge with the help of their dirks, the prickles being 'very uneasy to the loose-tailed lads', and, having fired, threw down their muskets and charged the dragoons, smiting at them with their swords. The dragoons were wearing iron skull-caps which gave them confidence, and unlike their comrades of Hamilton's and Gardiner's at Prestonpans they put up a stout resistance. Fourteen Highlanders broke their swords on the skull-caps but the remainder drove back the dragoons, first into the ditch – where for a time they had them almost at their mercy – and then

The Skirmish at Clifton – said to be the last battle on English soil

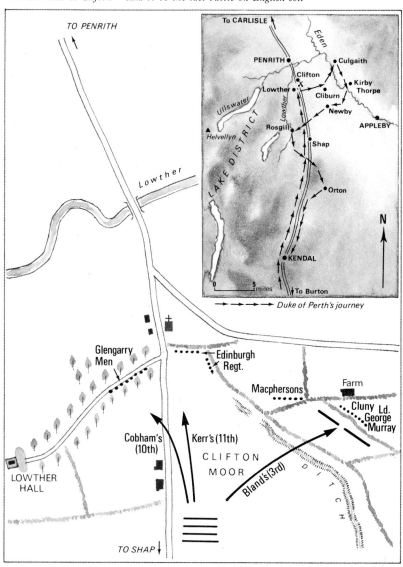

across the moor, while the Glengarries lining the wall of Lowther Park raked their flank. 'Colonel Honywood commanding Bland's, from neglecting to put on his skull cap, received three cuts on the head, and lost his sword to Cluny' who took it home as a trophy, and hung it in Cluny Castle, where it remained until transferred to the Clan Macpherson museum at Newtonmore. A dozen or so of Cluny's men disobeyed orders and crossed the ditch; five were killed and the rest taken prisoner. On the other side, Bland's suffered most casualties, having six killed.

This skirmish was to have sinister repercussions, for in writing his report Cumberland mentioned that, when some of the officers were wounded, the Highlanders had cried out, 'No quarter! Murder them!' and they had received several wounds after being knocked down. Prince Charles, however, was well pleased with what had happened at Clifton – in spite of his orders to withdraw being disobeyed – for it checked the pursuit and enabled the Highland army to reach Carlisle in safety.

Chapter VIII
STIRLING

'I have always been looked upon as a man of honour and you rebels will find that I shall die so.'

GOVERNOR BLAKENEY

On his return to Carlisle, Charles decided, against the advice of some of his commanders, to leave a garrison so as to retain a foothold on English soil, for he fully intended to resume the campaign in England when he had received the recruits assembled at Perth and the troops from France which had disembarked at Montrose. There was some difficulty in supplying a garrison, for the Highlanders were eager to get home and their chiefs were in sympathy, and not sanguine about the likely success of a renewed march southwards. But Colonel Townley's Manchester regiment had no desire to cross the Border, so he was willing to supply part of the garrison, and the residue was eventually drawn from the Duke of Perth's regiment and those of Lord Ogilvy, Gordon of Glenbucket and Roy Stewart. Colonel Strickland, who had come over on *Du Teillay*, was obliged to remain as he was suffering from dropsy and was too ill to proceed. Colonel John Hamilton was chosen as governor, and all the guns, except the Swedish cannon, were entrusted to him. The Highland army marched north on 20 December as far as Longtown on the English side of the Esk opposite Gretna, and there they halted until the whole force could come up and they were all ready to cross.

Meanwhile the Duke of Cumberland had spent the night of the skirmish at Clifton in a house in the village while his cavalry bivouacked on the moor. On the following day he went to Penrith and waited for his infantry to assemble. And on 21 December he marched his whole force in three columns towards Carlisle and closely invested the city. After a careful inspection he scornfully dismissed the castle as 'an old hen-coop which he would speedily bring down about their ears when he should have got artillery'. However, when his guns arrived they proved too small for the task of breaching the walls and he had to wait until 28 December for six 18-pounders to be brought up before he could carry out his threat. The garrison tried to hamper the men preparing earthworks for the cannon near Stanwix by continuous fire, but they did not achieve very much. Colonel Townley wanted to defend the castle to the last, but Governor Hamilton, realizing he had only a few days' supply of food, and would be heavily outgunned once the 18-pounders were emplaced, decided to parley. Having hoisted a white flag, he sent across a message asking that hostages might be exchanged, and complaining of the use of Dutch troops against him, contrary to recent Dutch treaties with France. This was a mistake as there were no Dutch involved; and it only resulted in a stiff note from the Duke stating he did not exchange hostages with rebels, and had no Dutch troops, 'only enough of the King's to chastise the rebels and those who dare give them assistance'. Two hours later Hamilton asked bluntly what terms the Duke would grant if the city and castle surrendered. Cumberland replied that the only offer he would or could make to the rebel garrison of Carlisle was that 'they shall not be put to the sword, but reserved for the King's pleasure'. This was not much; but it was something, and a surrender was agreed.

The garrison, including officers, consisted of 114 men of the Manchester regiment, 274 Scots mostly Lowlanders, and a few Frenchmen and Irishmen. The number of cannon was sixteen, ten of which had been left by the Highland army on its return to Scotland. Among the prisoners were twelve deserters from the royal forces who were immediately hanged. As a temporary measure, the officers were kept as prisoners in the castle and the men in the cathedral and town-gaol; afterwards all were dispersed in several gaols throughout England. The Duke of Cumberland left Bligh's regiment (20th) as a garrison at Carlisle, and then handed over the rest of his force to General Hawley, for there had been rumours of a possible French expedition, and the Government needed its most competent commander in the south where the invasion was expected.

At Longtown, where the Highland army was halted, the Esk was at least four feet deep at the crossing contemplated. However, it was tackled in a most systematic manner. To break the force of the current, and pick up any who might be washed off their feet, one body of cavalry rode in above the crossing and another below. Then the infantry dashed through in long lines of a hundred men abreast, holding on to each other, but leaving a gap before the next line for the free passage of the water. Lord George Murray who was one of the first across records that, on emerging and looking back, it seemed as if there were two thousand men in the water at once, for the space between the cavalry was one mass of bobbing heads. Everyone got across safely except two unhappy prostitutes who, not wanting to be left behind, bravely followed the men and were washed away and drowned. On reaching the far bank the pipers played and the men danced reels to dry themselves. Then they marched north in two columns, the one under the Prince going to Dumfries, and the other under Lord George Murray to Ecclefechan.[1]

The people of Dumfries were Government supporters and had appropriated thirty baggage-wagons left at nearby Lockerbie at the time of the invasion of England. Charles therefore demanded £2,000 compensation from its bailies and, it seems, was not over-censorious when his Highlanders did some pilfering in the town and neighbourhood, for an eye-witness records, 'At Dumfries they behaved very badly, stripped everybody almost of their shoes, obliged the town to give them £1,000 and carried away provost Crosbie and Mr. Walter Riddell as hostages for £1,000 more, which was yesterday sent them to relieve these gentlemen'.

From Dumfries Charles's army marched to Thornhill where the Prince set himself up at Drumlanrig Castle, the seat of the Duke of Queensberry whose ancestors had supported William of Orange and whose family was no friend of the Stuarts. According to the records, the Highlanders showed resentment here too, laying straw for beds in all the rooms except the Duke's chamber used by the Prince, and killing forty of the Duke's sheep inside the house next to the dining-room. They got into the cellars and drank or spilt most of the wine; they broke tables and chairs and defaced pictures; they melted down the pewter, and on leaving tried to make off with the blankets and linen until stopped by the Duke of Perth. One account ends plaintively, 'May God grant there may never again be any such guests here!'

The two columns reunited at Abington between Moffat and Douglas, and at the latter place the Prince stopped the night. The next night he stayed at Hamilton Palace, and enjoyed some sport on the following morning in the Duke's well stocked coverts. Meanwhile Lord Elcho's cavalry and Lord George Murray's column had gone on ahead and entered Glasgow, where the Prince joined them that evening, being escorted to his quarters at Shawfield House, Trongate by what, according to one eye-witness, seemed to be the bulk of his army.

The Prince treated the unfriendly townspeople of Glasgow with some severity. When told before the invasion of England to supply him with £15,000 they had sent only £5,500, and when asked for recruits, they had enlisted 700 Glasgow and Paisley men, put them under the command of Lord Home, and sent them to serve the Government in Edinburgh. The Highlanders were eager to plunder the city, and would have done so had they not been restrained by their chiefs. Cameron of Lochiel, for example, was so distressed that they might resort to such barbarism that he threatened to take his clansmen home. For this act of mercy Lochiel received the official thanks of the council and the promise that whenever the chief of Clan Cameron visited Glasgow in future the bells would be rung in welcome. Glasgow was spared a sacking, and instead a

1. Thomas Carlyle was born at Ecclefechan fifty years later.

88

peremptory order was sent to the Lord Provost telling him to deliver to the Highland army 12,000 shirts, 6,000 coats and waistcoats, 6,000 pairs of shoes and stockings, and 6,000 bonnets.

While the re-equipping of his army was proceeding, Charles lived in state at Shawfield House, and tried to woo the support of the gentlefolk of Glasgow by holding receptions for them and appearing at their social gatherings clad impressively in full court dress with insignia or in a handsome silken Highland costume. He also attempted to improve the morale of his army – and at the same time impress the citizens – by organizing a number of military parades. Almost every day a large detachment of Highlanders marched through the city, drums beating and bagpipes playing, and on 2 January, 1746, a major review was held on Glasgow Green.

As the days passed something akin to affection came to be felt for the Prince, if not for his soldiers, and many of the young ladies who served

Clementina Walkinshaw. After Allan Ramsay

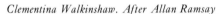

him at Shawfield House became highly enamoured, including particularly Miss Clementina Walkinshaw. Clementina's parents were both Jacobites, and her maternal grandfather was Sir Hugh Paterson at whose home, Bannockburn House, Stirling Charles stayed after leaving Glasgow, so there was an ample opportunity for them to meet daily for several weeks on end. Clementina's sister was a lady-in-waiting in the household of the Princess of Wales, and Clementina when staying with her had become versed in the manners of high society and court life – even if a rival court! Her love-affair with Charles is wrapped in a good deal of mystery and revealed only by a few cryptic, but by no means malicious, comments like 'the Prince was absent detained indoors by a cold, attended by his beloved Clementina'. To judge from a letter written from Boulogne it seems that it was in 1745 that she was in London, and, as she admits rather indelicately, in 1746 that she 'was undone'. Certainly there is no doubt about their being lovers, for later she bore him a child.

In November 1745 Lord John Drummond, brother of the Duke of Perth, had landed at Montrose with 800 men, consisting of his own Ecossais Royaux, detachments from all six regiments of the Irish Brigade (the Wild Geese) which was one of the *corps d'élite* of the French army, two squadrons of Fitzjames's regiment of horse and an artillery company with two 16-pounders, two 12-pounders and two 8-pounder guns which provided a valuable addition to Charles's train. Lord John also brought with him letters from the French king promising further support, and pointing out that, under recent French treaties agreed with the rulers of Nassau, Dutch troops could no longer be used by the British Government against the rebels. This particular communication was sent to Wade who passed it to the Duke of Newcastle in London for instructions, and in general Dutch troops were not subsequently used, being replaced by Hessians.

Drummond joined Lord Strathallan in trying to persuade the wavering chiefs of the north-east to support the Prince's cause. He failed in the case of his old friend Lord Fortrose, and also with the Duke of Gordon who pleaded illness and remained neutral. The latter's sailor brother Lord Lewis Gordon, however, was more co-operative and raised some Gordons in Aberdeenshire and Banff. Clan Chattan, although mainly sympathetic, was not completely involved. Some of the Farquharsons were out, and Cluny's Macphersons, in spite of Cluny having originally agreed to command one of the Government's independent companies; but the chief of the Mackintoshes, who also commanded a Black Watch company composed of his own clansmen, refused to resign his commission as Cluny had done. His wife Anne, who had been born a Farquharson, was however more enthusiastic. She rode around

Mackintosh territory clad in a riding-habit of tartan, and her appeal proved so irresistible that some 200 Mackintoshes and members of other local clans responded. This was the first time a clan had been raised by a woman, but it had the unfortunate effect of putting Mackintosh against Mackintosh.

Some of the Frasers, led by the Master of Lovat, were already under arms and they chose, as their first task, to try and take Fort Augustus. Hearing of this intention, the Campbell Lord Loudoun with men from his independent companies of loyal Highlanders marched south from Inverness to its relief. Lovat promptly raised the siege and led his men over the Corriearrack Pass to join Lord Strathallan at Perth, and so escaped. Loudoun stayed for a time in the neighbourhood of Fort Augustus and brought in sufficient supplies to last the garrison several months. Then, having warned the local people of the dire penalties they would incur if they molested the fort, or left their homes to support the Prince, he returned to Inverness. He had decided to pay the chief of the Frasers a visit and take him to task for allowing his son to go off with Fraser clansmen to join the Prince. On 8 December, 1745, he left Inverness with a reconstituted force for Dounie Castle,[1] the home of Simon Lovat. Lovat received his visitors cordially, and not only agreed to restrain the remainder of his clan, but to call in their arms. As a proof of his sincerity he agreed to accompany Loudoun back to Inverness and remain there until the arms were delivered. On 14 December when no arms had been sent in, Loudoun protested to Lovat, but the latter merely asked to be allowed a bit longer. A week later when still no arms had appeared, Loudoun with a guard of soldiers set out for Lovat's lodging, only to find he had gone. Apparently, during the night, a party of Frasers who had been hanging about Inverness quietly approached the back-door, and, as their chief was too infirm to walk, carried him off on their shoulders.

Loudoun was now joined by Macleod with a force of 400 of his clansmen from Skye and Assynt, and so was able to conduct his minor campaign in the north with more vigour. Hearing that Gordons were being raised by Lord Lewis Gordon at Aberdeen, Loudoun despatched the Macleods along with some men from his independent companies to try and prevent them leaving for the south. An advanced Gordon post at Fochabers on the Spey was relinquished as the force advanced, now accompanied by some Munroes who had joined them; but the Gordons, reinforced by a detachment of Lord John Drummond's men from Montrose, established a strong defensive position thirteen miles north-west of Aberdeen along the bank of the Don and Ure near Inverurie. The Inverness force lined the opposite banks of the two rivers and

1. *Twelve miles west of Inverness and now named Beaufort Castle.*

opened fire, and during the interchange both sides suffered casualties; but when the Gordons crossed over and attacked, their opponents fell back, first over the Spey, and the next day to Inverness, so the Gordons were after all allowed to proceed to Perth.

While Duncan Forbes and Lord Loudoun were trying to persuade the northern clans to stand firm, the Duke of Argyll had at last received permission to arm his Campbells in support of the Government. His kinsman General John Campbell of Mamore, who was fighting on the Continent, had offered his services, and been recalled to England to enroll and train an Argyll militia. It was not until 20 September, 1745, that he was definitely ordered to leave for Scotland, but his son Colonel John Campbell had started on the task of mustering his recruits before his father arrived. By 18 October, a few days before the official royal warrant was given to the Duke of Argyll as Lord Lieutenant, he had brought together three companies, and on 24 October the Duke of Newcastle authorized the supply of '500 muskets with ammunition in proportion and 500 broadswords to be sent from Liverpool by sea to Inverary for Colonel John Campbell'. After this auspicious start, however, the situation deteriorated. For one reason or another, but mainly owing to the lack of a suitable ship, General Campbell was delayed at Portsmouth for over a month and did not arrive until 21 December. And, even when he did reach Inverary, he suffered many frustrations. Despite continued pleas to the Government in London and to the Lord Lieutenant of Ireland he could not acquire sufficient oatmeal to feed his troops or enough weapons to equip them. Fortunately, he was an efficient organizer and trainer of men and, by the time the Prince reached Glasgow, had 2,000 Campbells under arms, 700 of whom he sent under his son John Campbell first to Dumbarton and from there to join General Hawley in Edinburgh.

All through November and December parties of Highlanders and men from the north-east outside the Highland line had been arriving in Perth, and together with Lord John Drummond's contingent from France some 4,000 were now assembled. Prince Charles had ordered Strathallan to join him before he invaded England, and was surprised when he had not done so; what he did not realize was that, on receipt of the Prince's instructions, Strathallan had called a council of war, and a majority of those present including Lord John Drummond had decided it was better to remain at Perth until Charles's return. The faction who had wanted to take part in the campaign then called a private meeting of their own at which it was decided to march off without further delay in accordance with the Prince's wishes; but Strathallan controlled the money and arms and ammunition without which it was impossible to leave. Even then some of the Highland regiments remained bent on

Perth

joining the Prince and were still seeking means to do so when the matter was resolved by the arrival of a messenger with the news that Charles's army had now returned to Scotland.

In the belief that nothing was to be gained by a longer stay in Glasgow, Charles decided, with the agreement of his commanders, to march east and join up with the reinforcements from Perth; after which, making use of the bigger guns brought from France, he proposed to attempt the reduction of Stirling, the possession of which would give him control of an important gateway to and from the Highlands. On reaching Stirling, he set up his headquarters at Sir Hugh Paterson's Bannockburn House, where he found Clementina Walkinshaw to greet him and give him comfort during his stay. Meanwhile, Lord George Murray sent the cavalry to reconnoitre towards Edinburgh and quartered the troops in Falkirk and neighbouring villages between that town and Stirling.

An attempt to persuade Stirling to capitulate was made the day after the army's arrival, when a drummer was sent with a message demanding the town and castle's surrender. As the drummer approached the main gate, however, militia sentries opened fire despite his protests that he was only a messenger, and the lad ran off leaving his drum which was then hooked up from the wall and taken as a trophy. As to the castle,

Governor Blakeney answered, 'I have always been looked upon as a man of honour and you rebels will find that I shall die so.' Next morning a trench was opened, and a battery emplaced within musket shot of the walls. The town was again summoned to capitulate and an answer demanded by two o'clock. It was a foregone conclusion. As Stirling was weakly fortified, with only some low fences and dry stone walls as protection, a prolonged resistance was out of the question, and after demanding and receiving, an extension of the time limit the town eventually surrendered.

The castle, however, was in a far stronger position. It was found necessary to bring the heavier guns up from Perth, and as Governor Blakeney had earlier destroyed one of the arches of Stirling bridge, this manoeuvre was by no means easy. In the end two guns were taken round by the west through the fords of Frew and the remainder brought to Alloa and ferried over the Forth. General Hawley attempted to stop them crossing the estuary by sending two naval sloops up river; but the Highland army set up batteries on the banks and drove off the warships. Charles chose an officer from France named Grant to conduct the siege operations against the castle, and the engineer selected a position for his batteries in Greyfriars churchyard opposite the main gate of the castle. However, before digging even began, townspeople living in the west end

Stirling Castle

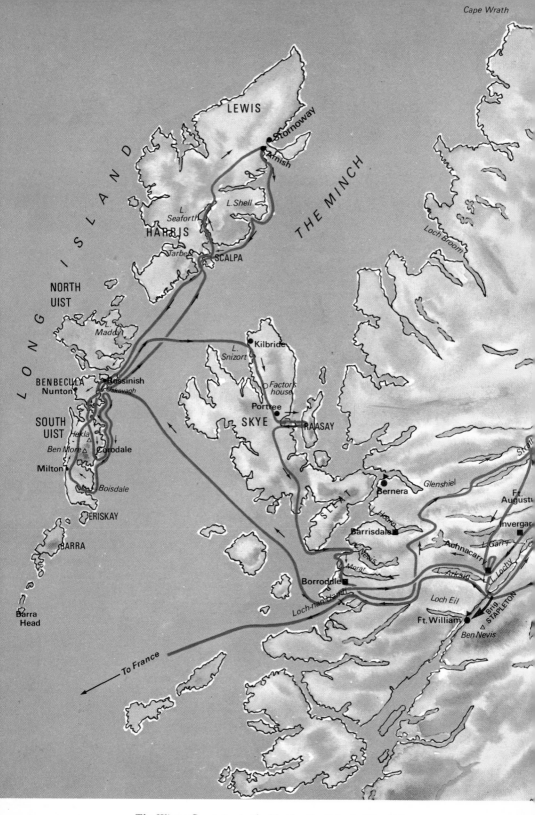

The Winter Campaign in the North: the Prince's Wanderings

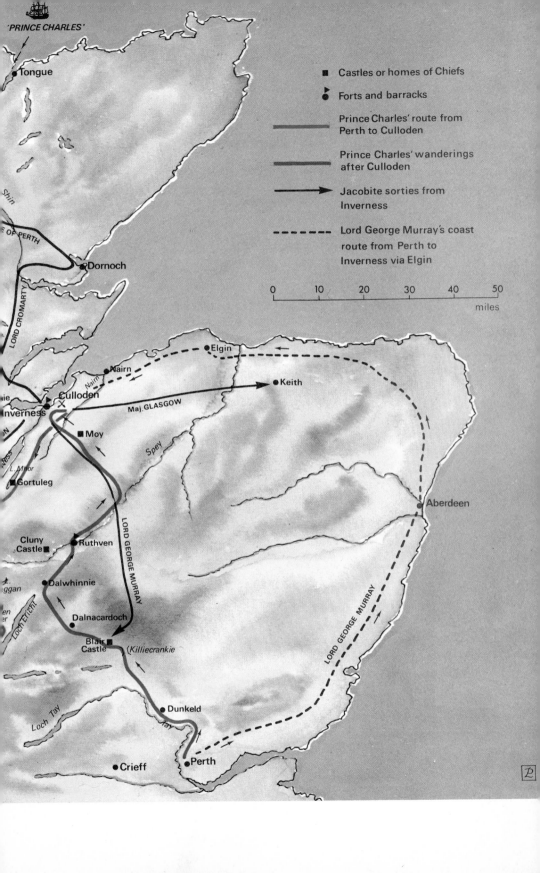

'PRINCE CHARLES'

Tongue

■ Castles or homes of Chiefs

▶ Forts and barracks

Prince Charles' route from
Perth to Culloden

Prince Charles' wanderings
after Culloden

Jacobite sorties from
Inverness

Lord George Murray's coast
route from Perth to
Inverness via Elgin

Shin

E OF PERTH

Dornoch

LORD CROMARTY

0   10   20   30   40   50
                                miles

Nairn

Elgin

Keith

Nairn

Culloden

Inverness

Maj. GLASGOW

■ Moy

Spey

L. Mhor

Gortuleg

Aberdeen

Cluny
Castle ■

Ruthven

LORD GEORGE MURRAY

Loch Ericht

Dalwhinnie

ggan

en
er

Dalnacardoch

Blair
Castle ■

(Killiecrankie

LORD GEORGE MURRAY

Loch Tay

Tay

Dunkeld

Crieff

Perth

complained that their houses would probably be destroyed by shells from the castle which passed over the battery, and the good-natured Prince agreed that another position for the battery should be selected. He ordered another engineer, Mirabelle, to take over, and the Frenchman selected a new site on a hill north of the castle. This was not an improvement; the soil was only fifteen inches deep and such additional protection as could be provided by sacks full of earth proved insufficient against the castle's fire which inflicted severe casualties among the gun detachments and the men doing the digging (these were drawn from the Irish picquets as the Highlanders considered such work beneath their dignity and, in any case, as had been found at Carlisle, were not good at digging trenches).

Very little had been accomplished at Stirling castle when news came that General Hawley was preparing to attack from Edinburgh. Hawley was a severe disciplinarian and thus a favourite of the Duke of Cumberland who used similar simple methods (these consisted in making sure that those who behaved well and fought staunchly were rewarded by promotion or gifts of guineas, while those who were recalcitrant and cowardly were flogged or hanged). At Sheriffmuir Hawley had been with the horse on the victorious right wing of Argyll's army and was convinced that Highlanders could not withstand a cavalry charge; he was said to boast that two regiments of dragoons could disperse a Highland army. He felt supremely confident as he rode out towards Falkirk with three regiments of horse, twelve of foot and ten guns.

Charles received the news of Hawley's approach with satisfaction. Since his arrival at Bannockburn, his army in spite of desertions had doubled in size, so he was able to leave a thousand under the Duke of Perth to continue the siege operations. The rest he drew up with the assistance of Colonel O'Sullivan in line of battle on Plean Moor ready to meet the enemy. This manoeuvre was repeated for several days in succession, and the Highlanders became so angry at being called out without any reason that they told their officers that, if it happened once more, they would go off on their own and attack the enemy. As a result a council of war was called, and when Lord George Murray suggested that as the enemy would not come to meet them they should advance and attack the enemy, everybody agreed; and the army, led by Murray himself, immediately started off in two parallel columns.

The main road from Bannockburn to Edinburgh passed through a remnant of old forest called Torwood, and then crossed the River Carron and a canal before reaching Falkirk. To the south of the road beyond some marshy ground lay Falkirk Moor, a hundred-foot-high plateau with a ravine in the centre of its northern slopes and a herdsman's hut and a few stonewall enclosures on its southern ones. Otherwise it was a stretch of open country. By the Carron south-east of Torwood,

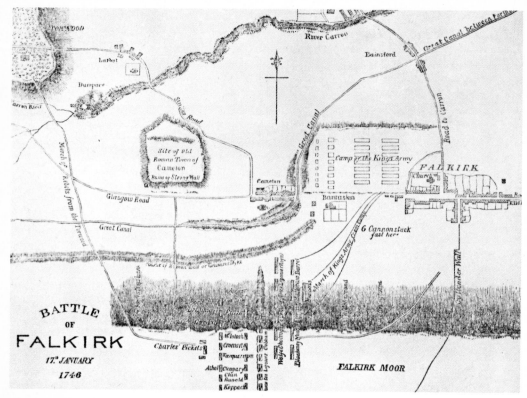

Plan of Falkirk, from Home's History

lay Dunipace House, where Charles's friend Sir Archibald Primrose
lived, and just to the east of Falkirk was Callendar House, the home of
Lord Kilmarnock, one of his cavalry leaders. Before the advance of the
Highland army General Hawley had established his army in a tented
camp north-west of Falkirk and his own headquarters at Callendar House
where, rather surprisingly, Lady Kilmarnock entertained him hospitably. North of the camp was a small hill, from the top of which was a
limited view of the area.

The Highlanders had expressed themselves eager for a fight, so Lord
George Murray decided to give them one as soon as possible; with this
in mind he made for Falkirk Moor, possession of which would be a
decided advantage. Hoping to delude the enemy as to the direction of
his attack, he sent the cavalry to create a diversion on the edge of Torwood where the Falkirk road left the forest, and then, without stopping
to co-ordinate a general plan, he led off the two columns round the south
of Torwood directly towards the moor. The Carron was swollen with

flood water and did not appear easily fordable, so Lord George called at Dunipace and asked where he could find the best crossing place. Sir Archibald Primrose suggested Dunipace Steps, and personally directed him there. At this stage the Prince, who was in the rear, came to the conclusion that it would be unwise to tackle the difficult crossing in the face of the enemy so late in the day, and he sent Colonel O'Sullivan with orders for Lord George Murray to wait until the following morning; but Lord George ignored the instruction, as he was to ignore so many others. The army forded the river without much difficulty at the place advised by Sir Archibald, and then, having crossed the canal and surmounted the grass-covered embankment of the old Roman wall, began to ascend the western slopes of the plateau.

Hawley did not expect the Highlanders to take the offensive. He thought rather that the Prince's army would occupy a defensive position near Bannockburn which could be attacked at leisure. No special precautions, therefore, were taken at the camp against surprise, and Hawley set about enjoying Lady Kilmarnock's lavish hospitality at well-warmed Callendar House without any concern. However, the day after their arrival at Falkirk there were rumours that the Highlanders were advancing, and Hawley rode with some of his officers to the top of the hill near the camp to investigate. Looking through their telescopes, the officers thought they could discern Highlanders north of Torwood; but Hawley insisted that he could see nothing, and returned happily to his comfortable quarters where he would be safe from the icy blasts. The next alert came at one o'clock when two officers climbed a tree on the observation hill and saw with the aid of their telescopes Highlanders debouching from the thickets of Torwood. It was now clear that instead of waiting on the defensive, as had been confidently believed, the Highlanders were advancing to attack. A courier took the news to Hawley who still remained unconvinced; but he did send back orders for his men to don their accoutrements. Soon afterwards, a mounted scout galloped back from his outpost and breathlessly announced that he had seen Highlanders fording the Carron at Dunipace Steps. This at last was enough, and the drummers immediately beat the men to arms. Without great speed – the men were at their dinners – the royal army formed up in two columns, and then, preceded by the cavalry, set off across the road to ascend the slopes of Falkirk Moor towards which the Highlanders could be seen marching. Hawley was even slower than his troops, and they were well under way before he arrived. He was flushed with the wine he had been partaking of too freely at dinner, and without his hat. In a state of excitement he rode to the head of his dragoons and roared out orders for them to gallop off to the summit of the plateau and forestall the Highlanders. Then, he put himself at the head of his infantry and led them up the hill. The weather, which had so far been fine, now changed for the worse; great storm clouds gathered in the south-west, the sky darkened, and a strong wind drove rain in the faces of the dragoons as they skirted the bog and galloped on up the hill. The regiments of foot followed in the wake of the horse, but the artillery found the ground on the borders of the bog too soft, and the guns stuck fast. The drivers, who were impressed civilians, after a few unsuccessful attempts to extricate the pieces, took out the horses and led them back to Falkirk, with the result that, as the Highlanders had no guns, the battle was fought without the use of artillery.

Charles's army approached in parallel columns, and on arriving at the summit of the plateau halted and faced left to form battle lines: the Macdonalds in their customary positions on the right, the Macphersons in the centre and the Stewarts of Appin and Camerons on the left. Before the battle began, Colonel O'Sullivan was sent by the Prince to organize the front line and co-ordinate the attack. He tried to persuade Lord George Murray to take advantage of the stone wall to his right front and the bog on his right, but Lord George considered the position of the Macdonalds, and his Athollmen behind, quite satisfactory, and refused to move. He was so eager to begin the fight that, as at Prestonpans, he gave little attention to any co-operation with the left. This, with Perth away, he assumed would be directed by Lord John Drummond.

The battle opened with the three dragoon regiments, Cobham's (10th), Ligonier's late Gardiner's (13th), and Hamilton's (14th), charging the Macdonalds without undue success. They galloped towards the Highlanders, halted and discharged their carbines, galloped forward to pistol range and halted again; but before they could fire, the Highlanders opened with their muskets, emptied many saddles and caused chaos in the ranks. Then, before the dragoons had time to rally, the Highlanders threw down their muskets, cast their plaids, unsheathed their swords and charged them. This was too much for Ligonier's and Hamilton's, who turned and galloped in panic to the rear, scattering Lord Home's Glasgow militia as they went. Cobham's men were stauncher. First they fought back, exchanging sword blow for sword blow. Then they veered right and rode off down the ravine which separated the front lines of the opposing armies on the other flank. Finally they rallied alongside Barrell's (4th) on the extreme right of the royal second line.

During this encounter between dragoon and Highlander both sides suffered casualties, and only by good fortune did Clanranald escape death. A dragoon's horse fell on him and pinned him to the ground, and he lay at the mercy of any passing assailant until a Highlander, engaged with a dismounted dragoon in single combat nearby, having killed his opponent, came to the chief's aid.

When the Highlanders charged in the centre, they met fully and squarely the royal infantry front line which turned and fled, Munro's (37th) among them. Sir Robert Munro had achieved so much with the Black Watch at Fontenoy that he had been given command of the 37th as a reward, and was at their head at Falkirk. They did not support him as the Black Watch had done. Instead, they left him to fight on alone along with his brother. Attacked by six Highlanders, he killed two with his half-pike;[1] but then received a pistol shot in the groin, and, as he fell, succumbed to a succession of sword blows. His brother was trying to come to his assistance when he was hit by a bullet in the chest, and seconds later he too was killed by a sword cut.

On the Highland right the Macdonalds had little in front of them once the cavalry had gone, and in the centre the royal regiments gave as the Highlanders charged; but on the left it was a different matter. Here the Stewarts and Camerons were on the opposite side of the ravine to Price's (14th), Ligonier's Foot (59th), and the Royal Scots, with Barrell's (4th) behind them; and although the Royal Scots gave, and also the Argyll Militia[2] in their right rear, the three other regiments along with Cobham's stood firm; and they not only drove the Camerons and Stewarts back over the ravine, but opened such a sustained fire in enfilade on the Highlanders at the centre as they pursued the royal infantry down the hill, that it halted them in their tracks. At this stage, Prince Charles attempted to rectify the position on the left by bringing forward the reserve lines. The Irish picquets advanced and countered the enfilade fire of Barrell's and the others sufficiently to allow the pursuit in the centre to continue; but they did not stop the Camerons and Stewarts drifting off disconsolately to the rear, as if they had been defeated.

The fog of war combined with the murk of the winter evening was such that few now knew what was happening. Many of the officers of the clans on the left had been deserted by their men who were straggling off home, and they now repaired to Dunipace House. Despondently, they crowded round the open fire and discussed the battle which they were fully convinced they had lost. On the right the Macdonalds had broken up into little knots and gone off down the hill quite out of control; but Lord George Murray was following with his Athollmen from the second line, and these were still well in hand. A halt was made when he reached the spot where Hawley's cannon were stuck in the bog. From there Lord George could see the three staunch royal foot regiments with Cobham's dragoons retiring down the road to Edinburgh in proper

1. *A spontoon.*
2. *Colonel John Campbell wrote: 'We had a skirmish yesterday evening. Our dragoons behaved very ill . . . our militia were not engaged but half of them dispersed and deserted.'*

military formation, ready to turn and fight a rearguard action if pressed. Barrell's had even got hold of ropes and manhandled a gun out of the bog, and they were dragging it away with them. It seemed that Hawley's whole force had not been routed, and when at this point the Prince joined Lord George Murray and the Athollmen, it was decided after a short discussion not to mount a full-scale pursuit, but instead to rally as many troops as possible, turn the enemy out of Falkirk, and spend the night there. As there would be some delay, a nearby hut on the moor was found to house the Prince, and Lord Kilmarnock was sent forward to reconnoitre in the neighbourhood he knew so well. When he re-appeared out of the gloom, he reported that the royal army had evacuated Falkirk, set fire to its camp and returned to Edinburgh.

Back at Dunipace House officers kept appearing, bringing contra-dictory reports, but no one knew what to believe until Lochgarry, leader of the Macdonells of Glengarry, who had lost his clan, arrived about eight o'clock and set everyone's minds at rest by announcing that the Prince had gained a decisive victory, and was at that moment safely quartered near Falkirk, while the discomfited Hawley was in full retreat with the remnants of his army. As Hawley's casualties numbered 400[1] while the Prince's barely exceeded 150, the Highlanders justly claimed a victory. The night after the battle was spent in looting the camp and stripping the bodies of the slain. The Highlanders added to the sinister reputation they had gained at Prestonpans where they had indiscrimi-nately killed the troops pressed up against Colonel Gardiner's park walls, and at Clifton Moor where they had said they would give no quarter, for next morning the whole face of the moor was clothed with naked corpses; to the inhabitants of Falkirk they seemed like a great flock of white sheep resting on the hillside, and on coming closer the terrible effects of claymore and dirk could be seen in the carpet of mutilated limbs and severed heads. Even while the looting was in progress, there was talk of following up Hawley's army and giving it the *coup de grâce;* but in the end it was decided that the capture of Stirling castle was more important, so while the bulk of the army remained in the villages around Falkirk, the Prince returned to Bannockburn House to wait for the Duke of Perth to carry the siege operations to a successful conclusion.

1. *Home, 300–400 killed; Kirkconnel, 400–500 killed; Johnstone, 600 killed and 700 prisoners; official returns 280 casualties.*

Chapter IX

INVERNESS

'The rebels give out that he is every day hunting and hawking at Blair, which does not seem at all suited to his inclinations; for he can hardly sit on horseback and therefore made all his marches on foot.'

CUMBERLAND IN A LETTER TO THE
DUKE OF NEWCASTLE

Charles was suffering from a very severe cold caught while sleeping out in the hut on Falkirk moor, so he stayed indoors at Bannockburn House. Here he had the compensation of being tended by Clementina Walkinshaw who declared she loved him so dearly that she would follow him wherever he went; she kept her promise, for she later joined him in France. The Prince had intended to go over to Falkirk and review his troops who very much needed his inspiring presence as they had grown impatient at waiting for the end of the siege and started to desert in substantial numbers. His persistent cold, however, prevented him, with disastrous consequences.

After a week or so, news arrived that Cumberland was coming to Edinburgh to take over command, and Charles decided that rather than wait to be attacked it would be better to go over to the offensive. He sent Murray of Broughton with a message to Lord George Murray at Falkirk asking for the general's view and enclosing a suggested plan of attack. To his surprise, Lord George agreed and returned a modified plan for the Prince's formal approval. Charles was just congratulating himself that he had at last obtained the co-operation of his difficult subordinate, when a second message arrived from Lord George completely at variance with the first and not only ignoring the previous plans, but suggesting instead an immediate retreat to the Highlands. This was only the last of a series of difficulties with the commanders, and particularly with Lord George Murray who was always challenging the Prince's orders; but because it was so sudden a reversal of the previous day's agreement the Prince was more upset than before. 'Good God! Have I lived to see this?' he exclaimed; and in his anger flung himself about so uncontrolledly that he struck his head against the wall of his room and momentarily stunned himself

The course of events which led to this *volte-face* on the part of the

Prince's senior general seems to have been as follows: Lord George Murray had called a council of war of the principal commanders at Falkirk, and their general view was that, owing to wholesale desertion, the Highland army was no longer in a fit state to engage the enemy in the Stirling area. As there seemed no chance of taking Stirling castle except by starving out the garrison, which would take months and produce even larger-scale desertions, it would be wiser to retreat to the Highlands. These points were embodied in a memorial sent to the Prince, along with some suggestions for subsequent operations to occupy the army during the winter months. After stressing that they had tried hard but with no avail to stem the desertions, and reiterating that it would be foolish to engage the enemy with Stirling castle held by Government troops in their rear, the chiefs suggested that the rest of the winter should be occupied in taking Inverness, Fort Augustus and the other Government-held forts in the Highlands; and for this sufficient Highlanders would be kept under arms. If a French landing occurred in the meantime a stronger force would be embodied, and in the spring a new army of 10,000 would be raised to continue the campaign which had been temporarily suspended. The memorial was signed by Lord George Murray, Donald Cameron of Lochiel, the Macdonald chiefs Keppoch and young Clanranald, Cluny Macpherson, the Master of Lovat representing the Frasers in the field, Ardshiel commanding the Stewarts of Appin, and Glengyle the leader of the Macgregors. To soften the blow the chiefs said that although they were asking the Prince to retire beyond the Forth, they still meant to stand by him, 'and the glorious cause we have espoused to the utmost of our lives and fortunes'.

Charles soon recovered from his angry mood. Remembering Derby, he came to see that as all the principal clan leaders had signed the memorial, he would have to let them have their way. But he was determined not to yield without a protest, and he sent back by Sir Thomas Sheridan a reasoned answer to their suggestions. He asked whether Falkirk had meant nothing, for why retreat after a victory? Would they be likely to do better at Perth, or in the Highlands where it would be difficult to stop desertions with the men so near their homes? Would the French and Spanish support them if they retired? Was it fair to desert the Lowlanders, or ask them to march into the mountains? He ended by emphasizing how reluctant he was to agree to a retreat, and by inviting the chiefs to talk over the situation with Sir Thomas Sheridan who knew his views. This appeal resulted in the appearance of Keppoch and Cluny; but the discussion that followed only caused a further display of pique on the part of the Prince, and his eventual surrender to the inevitable. In a final message to his chiefs he wrote: 'After all this I know I have an army that I cannot command any further than the chief officers please, and therefore if you are all resolved upon it I must yield; but I take God to witness that it is with the greatest reluctance, and that I wash my hands of the fatal consequences which I foresee but cannot help.'

The retreat was a sadly botched affair. Left on his own, its chief architect Lord George Murray might very well have organized it expeditiously; but although it had been agreed to assemble at nine o'clock next morning, directly the siege was abandoned the Duke of Perth, Lord John Drummond and all the troops in and around Stirling, in the firm belief that departure was urgent in case they were pursued and caught by the enemy, abandoned their posts and their stores, and started for the north at daybreak as an undisciplined mob. The assembly place had been St. Ninian's, two miles south of Stirling, three miles north of Bannockburn House and ten miles from the camps of the main army around Falkirk. When the Prince arrived there were very few men about, so having given orders for the gunpowder stored in the church to be removed and destroyed, he took the Dumbarton road, and with his followers rode off north in the wake of Perth's men. Some of the gunpowder had already

Charles after his return to France. Engraving after Quentin de La Tour

been taken out of the church and spilled. Then it was noticed that villagers were attempting to pilfer powder and other stores, and a sentry fired a warning shot to frighten them off. Sparks from the discharge of his musket ignited the loose powder, the flames moved towards the church and the remaining barrels exploded. It happened just when the wounded Donald Cameron of Lochiel and Mrs. Murray of Broughton were driving through the village in a chaise. The explosion wrecked the church completely except for the tower, killed fourteen or fifteen by-standers, and caused the horses of Lochiel's carriage to bolt and tip out Mrs. Murray into the road, though fortunately without any serious injury to the lady.

When Lord George Murray reached St. Ninian's, he gazed upon a scene of indescribable confusion, for the men from Falkirk on arriving at the rendezvous had not waited for the organization of an orderly retirement but had merely followed the fleeing Stirling men in a similar state of tumult. In his memoirs he wrote later: 'At a distance the men were running off as if an enemy were in pursuit of them . . . there were none belonging to the army at Ninian's; but the ruins of the church were to be seen and many country people gathered about the place, for it was an hour and a half after it was blown up . . . it was by no means a retreat but a flight; the men were going off like so many sheep scattered upon the side of a hill, or like a broken and flying army after a defeat and hot pursuit.'

By the time Crieff was reached, however, some sort of order was restored. To consolidate this the Prince held a review of the troops in the vicinity, and he was surprised to discover that the desertions at Stirling and Falkirk could not have been on anything like the scale he had been led to believe. Instead of two or three thousand, only about one thousand were missing, and he was forced to the conclusion that Lord George Murray and the chiefs had exaggerated in order to persuade him to agree to the retreat. He certainly now suspected the integrity of his senior general.

Lord George Murray, for his part, was furious over the chaos of the retreat which he had advised. It had been so disorganized as to give the impression to the enemy that the rebels were in panic-stricken flight; and Lord George asked that a council of war should be called to investigate the matter. It was held in a room of the Drummond Arms, Crieff, and the Prince found it as unpleasant as the one at Exeter House, Derby had been. Everyone realized that the disorderly retreat from Stirling had dealt a blow to the prestige of the Jacobite army. Cameron of Lochiel felt this most strongly, and his reaction was shared by Lord Elcho whose troop had not been notified of the withdrawal and had narrowly escaped capture by Cumberland's army moving west from Edinburgh. It seemed to Lord George in the preliminary discussion as if his fellow commanders were blaming him for the catastrophe, but this he would not accept. White with anger, he took the chair at the council. His main object was to find who was responsible for altering the time of the start and, so as to ensure that this was kept in mind, he refused to let anyone speak unless called upon. According to Colonel O'Sullivan, 'Lord George would not allow anyone to speak but those he named, and when the Prince attempted to speak, he threatened to leave, and told the Prince he must not speak until everyone had given his opinion.' Lord Lewis Gordon asked if Lord George were mad, for surely the Prince their master could speak when he thought fit; but his protests did not deflect Lord George from his purpose. 'Will your Royal Highness name who gave this pernicious advice?' he demanded angrily. 'I am afraid we have been betrayed, for it is worth the Government in London £100,000 to any who would have given such advice and get it followed.' O'Sullivan roundly swore he was not responsible. Then the Prince firmly declined to name anybody, and even took the blame upon himself. There was no more to be said, and the council was at last able to discuss more important matters such as the route to be taken northwards.

Even this, however, was not decided without wrangling and altercation. The Prince wanted to go by the coast and Aberdeen so that his army would be in touch with any French troops who might land; the chiefs on the other hand preferred to take the direct route to the Highlands in order to get home as soon as possible. Eventually it was decided that the horse and Lowland regiments should follow the coast road while the Prince at the head of the clans should take the direct road north. Lord George, after the other officers refused, agreed to lead the column going round by the coast; and he allowed young Lord Ogilvy, who wished to leave his wife at his Forfar home, to go directly there with his men. So, in the end, there were three columns.

The Duke of Cumberland had followed reasonably quickly as far as Stirling, but he was held up by the impassable state of the bridge which had earlier been blown up by Governor Blakeney to impede the Highland army. Thus the rebel columns could proceed northwards unimpeded. The coast column in particular had an uneventful march, though wintry conditions on the last stage made progress slow. When they reached Elgin they were joined by 600 Deeside men, and Lord George put these and his own troops into winter quarters in the neighbourhood and rode off to join the Prince and discover how the clans had fared in their march over the hills. Charles, meanwhile, had proceeded leisurely, stopping on the way at the homes of his friends, first at the Duke of Perth's Castle Drummond beyond Dunblane, then at Castle Menzies and finally at Blair Castle where he was entertained again by his old comrade-in-arms Tullibardine. Tullibardine had gone north before the battle of Falkirk to raise more of his people. But, although they still thought of him as their Duke, his recruiting drive produced poor results. The Athollmen, many of whom had already deserted from both sides, were not enthusiastic. 'I am sorry to tell you,' Tullibardine wrote to a friend, 'that instead of three or four regiments, there are hardly men enough come together to make up one.'

While he was still at Blair Castle, Charles learnt that Cumberland's advanced guard, consisting of Colonel John Campbell's Argyll militiamen, had invaded ducal territory near Dunkeld. Hoping the presence of the hated Campbells and the thought of action against them might encourage his men to take up arms, Tullibardine suggested that an attempt should be made to hold Killiecrankie Pass and oppose the advance of the royal army there; but the Prince disallowed this plan, on the grounds that the Campbells being Highlanders would fight as well in the hills as his own men. In spite of all these problems, though, Charles managed to enjoy a day's hunting in the forests round the castle. His cousin Cumberland sneered when he heard of it. In a letter to the Duke of Newcastle, he remarked, 'The rebels give out that he is every day hunting and hawking at Blair, which does not seem at all suited to his inclinations; for he can hardly sit on horseback and therefore made all his marches on foot.'

Meanwhile, the advanced troops of the Prince's column had passed through Dalnacardoch and Dalwhinnie, and on 7 February reached Ruthven in the upper valley of the Spey. Ruthven was still manned by the same small garrison under Molloy which had held out so gallantly earlier. Molloy, indeed, had been promoted lieutenant because of his staunch resistance. Now, however, the situation was different. Instead of hundreds there were thousands of Highlanders surrounding his barracks. Realizing that resistance was hopeless he agreed to capitulate on condition that he and his men were given passes to take them through enemy-held territory. This was granted with the stipulation that they should bind themselves on oath not to serve under arms against the Prince for two years, and Molloy and his garrison marched away. A considerable amount of meal and some barrels of gunpowder were found in Ruthven. The hungry Highlanders scrambled for the meal without waiting for its proper distribution; and the powder was used to blow up the barracks. The Prince did not linger but pressed on to Moy, nine miles from Inverness. Here the Highlanders were cantoned in neighbouring villages, and Charles himself was entertained at Moy Hall by Lady Anne Mackintosh who had been so spirited in raising men of the clan.

Lord Loudoun was at Inverness with a number of Government Highland companies; Wade's castle was manned by some regular troops, and there were also sixteen cannon, plenty of ammunition and ample provisions in the fortress. When Loudoun heard that Charles was at Moy Hall a few miles away with only a small bodyguard, he decided to try and capture him. At midnight on 16 February he set off for the Hall at the head of 1,500 Government Highlanders with some Macleods in the van. But, in spite of efforts to keep the mission a secret, the Dowager Lady Mackintosh who lived in Kirk Street, Inverness heard of Loudoun's design, and despatched a lad to warn Charles. The boy followed in the rear of Loudoun's column until it reached a fork in the road. When the column chose the longer though better road to Moy, the boy took the more direct route across the moor and reached the Hall in time to warn the sentries guarding the Prince. They roused the household, and, true to form, Lady Anne Mackintosh quickly took charge. She armed four of her servants with loaded muskets and sent them out under the local blacksmith Donald Fraser to watch for the approach of Loudoun's column; she then despatched the Prince with his bodyguard of thirty Highlanders to hide in a thick wood a mile away by Loch Moy.

Lady Mackintosh's men served the Prince well. Stopping short of a dip in the road, and peering into the dim light of the early morning, they saw against the skyline a large body of men moving towards them. The blacksmith fired his musket, and with his first shot killed Donald Bau Maccrimmon[1] the celebrated Macleod piper from Skye. Then the four servants fired, the blacksmith, meanwhile, yelling orders as if he were commanding a thousand men instead of four, and calling to the Macdonalds, 'Advance, advance, my lads! I think we have the dogs now!' and to other imaginary clansmen, 'Charge on the left, Camerons!' What with the war cries and the flashes of the muskets, Loudoun's men were convinced they had run head-on into the Highland army, and the five rear companies turned about and fled towards Inverness. Loudoun, seeing the panic and confusion even among the stauncher men who remained, then also withdrew to Inverness.

Charles returned to Moy Hall considerably the worse from his night in the woods, for he contracted another severe cold which kept him indoors for several weeks and made it impossible for him to take an active part in the operations during the early months of 1746. The Highland army, however, pressed on to Inverness and found that Duncan Forbes, Loudoun and Macleod and their men had crossed the Firth by the ferry to Kessoch, in order to avoid a battle and await the arrival of Cumberland in friendly territory. The castle, however, still held out with its garrison of eighty of Guise's regiment (6th) to which Loudoun before his departure had added a company of Grants and a

---

1. *Maccrimmon was a member of a family of hereditary pipers who for some centuries were attached to the household of the Macleods of Dunvegan in Skye. A presentiment of his fate inspired him to compose before he left Skye the beautiful and pathetic lament, 'Cha till me tuille' (I'll return no more').*

company of Macleods. When summoned to surrender Major Grant refused to do so, and the Prince, by now recovering from his cold, ordered the siege operations to be started. The castle was close to the buildings of the town and its walls could be approached under cover from the garrison's fire, so mines were laid in position beneath the main bastions on the north side next to the town. A few shots were exchanged with the garrison, but before the mines were blown Major Grant surrendered. To gratify the Highlanders, who regarded Government fortresses in their territory with aversion, Charles ordered the French soldiers to explode the mines directly the garrison had been marched out as prisoners. The mines duly went off and completed their task, except for the last one near the bridge. When the sergeant who had directed the operation ran forward to investigate, just as he was stooping to examine the train, the explosion occurred, and he was shot into the air and fell in the river, from where his dead body was afterwards recovered.

During the early months of 1746, before the approach of Cumberland, operations were carried out in all directions from Inverness. One expedition was against the Government Highlanders who had fled to friendly Mackay and Sutherland country in the north, other sorties were aimed at the Government-held fortresses of Fort Augustus and Fort William. Lord George Murray even staged his own assault on his old home Castle Blair which was now in Government hands. With the Prince's permission he set off with some of his own men and Cluny's Macphersons to attempt to oust an Argyll militia detachment. As he possessed no battering-ram, and his small field-pieces made no impression on the castle's seven-foot-thick walls, he attempted a blockade. On 2 April, however, before the garrison had made any offer to surrender, he was recalled to Inverness where news had arrived that the army of the Duke of Cumberland was on the march.

The Duke of Perth and Lord John Drummond now began to carry out delaying operations on the Spey in the path of Cumberland's leading columns. The first of these was a minor triumph. Major Glasgow, an Irish Officer in the French service, with 200 foot and forty horse crossed the Spey after dark and stormed an Argyll militia post in Keith, a town a few miles east of the river. A detachment of Campbells was in a church, and when the alarm was given they manned the churchyard and opened fire on Glasgow's men. After the engagement had proceeded for some time, Glasgow offered them generous terms if they would surrender, and as Captain Campbell their commander had been killed along with six of his men, the survivors laid down their arms.

The operations in the north were only partially successful. Initially they were under the direction of Lord Cromarty, who took with him some Jacobite Mackintoshes and some Macgregors, but he did not seem to be making much progress so Lord George Murray went north to

Fort George, Inverness, destroyed by Prince Charles. The new Fort George is several miles to the east

investigate. He reported bluntly that Cromarty 'was doing no good', and the Duke of Perth with a detachment of Macdonalds were sent to replace him. Perth acted with more vigour. He drove the Government Highlanders from Dornoch north-westwards up Loch Shin, and after a chase of thirty miles halted his men at the head of the Loch. During the night pursuit the Macdonalds were worried because they might be confused with the Macdonalds from Skye on the opposing side. This was because all the Macdonalds wore as a distinguishing mark a bit of heather[1] in their bonnets.

Although the Government Macdonalds and the Macleods escaped to Skye,[2] Charles appeared pleased with these events and sent a letter to France by Captain Warren, an Irishman, to tell his friends there, so that they might try to persuade Louis XV to send additional help; though in fact the *Prince Charles* with £13,000 in gold and some Irish picquets had already left for Scotland under the command of Captain Richard Talbot, another Franco-Irishman, who had served with Antoine Walsh on the *Du Teillay*.

1. Yew was worn be the Frasers, oak by the Camerons, holly or wild thyme by the Drummonds, box by the Mackintoshes, red whortleberry by the Macphersons and thistle by the Stewarts.
2. On reaching western Sutherland, Forbes, Loudoun and Macleod, along with 800 Macdonalds and Macleods, marched to the coast and took ship for Skye, while the officers and men of Forbes's regiment of mixed clans took refuge in friendly Mackay country towards Cape Wrath.

With the Prince's headquarters at Inverness, and Cumberland now at Aberdeen, Talbot decided to try and land between them at Portsoy, on the shores of Banff. After first being driven back to Ostend by a British privateer the remainder of the voyage was uneventful until they approached the Banff coast, where Talbot came upon Commodore Smith's squadron of two battleships and two sloops, and quickly decided to run north to the Pentland Firth. The twenty-four gun *Sheerness* gave chase, but Talbot crowded on sail and the *Prince Charles* got away. She had passed through the Firth, entered Tongue Bay, and was just approaching the shore, when the *Sheerness* hove in sight again. Talbot clewed up the *Prince Charles*'s sails and, when the ship touched bottom on sand near the mouth of the bay, dropped anchor to hold position so as to fire a broadside against the *Sheerness*, now herself anchored half a cannon shot off-shore. The *Prince Charles* was heavily out-gunned, but took a long time to die. It was not until evening when most of the guns were out of action and thirty-eight sailors and fifteen men of the Irish picquets had been killed that it was decided to abandon ship and proceed to Inverness with as much gold as the men could carry.

At first they were in luck, for the house they approached belonged to a Mackay laird friendly to the House of Stuart. He told them that two Government Highland companies and a hundred men of Loudoun's regiment were in the neighbourhood, and Inverness was eighty miles or more away through hostile country. They bought two horses from the laird to carry the gold, and having destroyed all the letters and despatches they carried, set off for Inverness with the laird's son as their guide.

After this their fortune changed. The *Sheerness* sent news of their landing to Lord Reay, the old chief of the hostile Mackays, who called together the Government Highlanders in the neighbourhood and staged an ambush for the little band on the road south. When they found themselves surrounded, Talbot's men drew up and made a brave attempt to resist capture, but their few muskets made a poor reply to the volleys that came in on them from all sides, and after several men had been killed or wounded, the rest surrendered: according to Talbot, Lord Reay received them '*avec beaucoup d'humanité et de politesse*'. In order to ensure that the gold was not recaptured or the prisoners released by the Highland forces at Loch Shin, Reay had the men and the money taken aboard the *Sheerness*, which, after first floating and securing the *Prince Charles* as a prize,[1] set sail for Aberdeen.

The Highland operation against Fort Augustus was conducted by Brigadier Stapleton with the Ecossais Royaux and his Irish picquets.

1. *The Royal Navy was particularly pleased to take this sloop, for as the* Hazard *it had been captured at Montrose by the French with the help of men of the Prince's army.*

6. CULLODEN.

Without waiting for the arrival of his artillery, Stapleton sent in his troops against the barracks and drove the three companies of Guise's Regiment into the fort. Grant had once again taken over as chief engineer from Mirabelle, and he emplaced his guns and opened fire. After two days of bombardment he was lucky enough to hit and explode the fort's main powder magazine, on which the senior officer Major Wentworth agreed to surrender. The operations against Fort William which followed were, however, less successful because of its energetic defence by Captain Caroline Scott. Although the fortifications were in bad repair, work was at once put in hand to strengthen them; Scott had a quantity of artillery and ammunition, and additional fire support from naval vessels lying alongside the fort in Loch Linnhe. The garrison consisted of 200 men of Guise's and some Argyllshire militia, and they all fought bravely.

Brigadier Stapleton was again in charge of the siege operations, but he set up his batteries on Sugar Loaf Hill which was too far away, and his shells consequently did little damage to the fort. The counter-battery fire was more effective, for the pieces in the fortress, supplemented by the guns on the ships, at one stage put out of action most of Stapleton's artillery. After two days Stapleton hopefully sent across a letter summoning the garrison to surrender, but this was met with an answer from Scott that he would receive no letters from rebels and would hold the fort to the last. Cannonading continued for a week, day and night, and then, making use of the moonlight, Scott organized two sallies; the first charged the battery, drove off the French gunners, and captured and carried away the small guns and spiked the large ones; while the second saw off a body of infantry advancing in support. Then, when Stapleton was seen organizing a more massive counter-attack, Scott showed he could be wary as well as active, for he called his men in. For two days more the Jacobite force carried out a spasmodic bombardment, but then, feeling the situation was hopeless, having spiked the five remaining serviceable guns in the battery, they withdrew. The bright moonlight had made it impossible to surprise the garrison by night, and the siege had not been well conducted; but Captain Scott for his part had shown vigour and resource and deserved the commendation of King George 'who looked upon the raising of the siege as greatly owing to the courage and good conduct of Captain Scott, whose behaviour has given His Majesty great satisfaction'. In accordance with Cumberland's methods, Major Grant the commander of Stirling castle and Major Wentworth of Fort Augustus were cashiered, but Captain Scott was promoted.

Chapter X

CULLODEN

'For once the bayonet, used in the manner in which they
had been trained, gained the advantage for the royal
soldiers over the Highlanders' broadsword.'

At Aberdeen, Cumberland assembled an impressive fleet of transports
to carry the warlike stores he required to maintain his army during his
march on Inverness and his subsequent operations in the Highlands;
and on 8 April, when all was ready, and the weather improved, preceded
by his cavalry and the Campbell scouts, he set out. His column of some
9,000 men was made up of Cobham's and Kerr's dragoons, Kingston's
volunteer light horse, fifteen regiments of foot and an efficient artillery
train of sixteen guns under Colonel Belfort. They were quartered on the
first night at Meldrum, and on the second at Banff, where two spies
were seized and hanged, one having been caught notching a stick with
the number of the Duke's forces. On 12 April they approached Fochabers six miles from the Spey, and formed up in three divisions to cross
the river in different places. As they marched they had been comforted
by seeing the transports and accompanying warships from Commodore
Smith's squadron sailing close inshore alongside them. When one ship
opened fire on the Duke of Perth's cavalry beyond the Spey, they gave a
hearty cheer. Perth and Lord John Drummond had 2,500 men on the
far side of the river, and had they offered opposition it could have made
the crossing difficult; but they had been ordered to fall back unless
reinforced, and did nothing to hinder the royal army. Although the
river was in flood and the water reached the men's waists even in the
shallowest places, only one dragoon and four women were carried
away by the stream and drowned, and the rest passed over safely. On
14 April the port of Nairn was reached, and the Duke of Cumberland
set up a massive tented camp to house his men, with the intention of
staying there, at least over his twenty-fifth birthday which was on the
following day.

Cumberland was both respected and feared: respected because of his
achievements as commander-in-chief in Flanders; feared because he
had approved Hawley's hangings, and was known to employ similar
methods. Although nothing had happened to counter their last humiliat-
ing defeat at Falkirk, the regiments were in surprisingly good heart, and

Tortoiseshell snuffbox set with a portrait miniature of Cumberland painted by Christian Friedrich Fricke. Presented to Lieutenant-Colonel George Howard who commanded the 3rd of Foot (Buffs) in the second line at Culloden

Barrell's particularly so. Because of their staunch resistance when so many took to their heels, and their skilful removal of one of the guns from the mire, they had not only been publicly commended but rewarded also by a gift of guineas. Cumberland's birthday was used by him as a means of raising his men's spirits still higher. At his own expense he issued an anker of brandy to each battalion of his army, and bread and cheese too, and meat from the bullocks driven up from the Spey. He rode round and greeted his troops as they celebrated with him, raising his hat in answer to their complimentary cries of 'Flanders! Flanders!' and saying, 'My brave boys, we have but one march more and all our labour is at an end. Sit down at your tent doors and be alert to take up your arms.'

The news that Cumberland's army had crossed the Spey reached Inverness on 13 April, and the Highland troops in the area were immediately called to arms. After being addressed by the Prince, they marched out of the town, pipes playing, until they reached nearby Culloden House which had been chosen as a rendezvous. During the evening Lochiel and his Camerons arrived, having covered the fifty miles from Fort William in two days; later the Duke of Perth and the advanced forces from the Spey came in; and the Frasers were reported on the way. But Cluny's Macphersons were still in the south having left Castle Blair after Lord George Murray and stopped in the Ruthven area; and the Mackenzies, Macgregors and M'Donells of Barrisdale were in the far north, having been sent back to try and recover the gold brought over on the *Prince Charles*. Owing to the loss of this £13,000 the Prince had been forced to pay his men in oatmeal instead of coin. Murray of Broughton, his secretary, was ill and the administrative arrangements were left in the hands of John Hay of Restalrig who found the task too much for him. The result was that the arrangements for bringing the meal from Inverness to Culloden broke down; the hungry Highlanders had set off in search of the meal, or substitute rations, and many were absent from their bivouacs around Culloden, and were not easily mustered for subsequent operations. In theory, counting only legitimate absentees, the Prince's army should have numbered 7,000, but with so many away foraging it seldom exceeded 5,000.

On 14 April a general battle order was issued to the principal commanders stating that every man must join a unit and stay with it until the end of the battle; any who turned their backs and deserted would be shot; and stripping the slain and plundering were forbidden until the battle was over. It has been asserted that a copy of this order taken from a captured Highlander had the additional words 'and give no quarter to the Elector's troops'; but the few copies still in existence do not include this sinister sentence which was later made use of by Cumberland to justify his reprisals.

On the following day, believing that Cumberland's army was about to attack, the Prince gave instructions for his army to be drawn up by Colonel O'Sullivan to receive the enemy on Culloden Moor, with its left protected by a bog and its right by the River Nairn. Such a disposition did not meet with the approval of Lord George Murray who believed the open moor, in spite of its irregularities and marshy patches, would favour the enemy. He wanted a move to be made towards the hilly ground beyond the Nairn, but the Prince and the majority of the commanders present at the discussion were of the opinion that if the Highland army went so far away, Cumberland would merely ignore them, march on Inverness and seize their baggage and stores. Charles did, however, agree to allow Brigadier Stapleton the commander of the Irish picquets, and Colonel Ker, who had done such useful reconnaissance work at Prestonpans, to ride out and inspect the country beyond the Nairn. They later reported the area favourable, but by that time a position on the moor had definitely been decided on.

When it became apparent that Cumberland would not attack after all, someone volunteered the information that it was his twenty-fifth birthday and the day was being spent in celebrations by the royal army at Nairn. When this had been confirmed the men were sent back to continue their foraging, and Charles and his staff rode out to Kilravock to undertake a reconnaissance. At a council of war on their return to Culloden House, the Prince suggested that as there seemed no chance of Cumberland attacking immediately, they should attack him instead. At first there was little support for the idea, but when Lord George – who felt that anything would be better than waiting to fight on 'that plain muir' – gave his support, the others agreed. The clans, he suggested, should march at dusk that day, pass round the town of Nairn in the darkness and fall upon the royal soldiers while they were drunk, as drunk they surely would be after celebrating their commander's birthday. One far-seeing chief objected that as he did not propose to march from Culloden until dusk, the army would not complete the march before daylight; but Lord George confidently replied he would 'answer for it'.

Before the depleted columns marched off – many men were still absent foraging – the Prince rode up to the front and, putting his arm round Lord George Murray, affectionately thanked him for agreeing to lead the night march; but Lord George did not respond to his master's gesture of reconciliation, merely raising his bonnet, and making a stiff bow.

Things began to go wrong almost from the start. The Mackintoshes were chosen to lead as the area bordered their own country, and they and the Camerons, although the latter had hardly recovered from their long march from Fort William, set too fast a pace for the encumbered Irish picquets and the Lowland regiments behind; scarcely a mile was covered when the first of many messages reached Lord George asking him to set a slower pace as the rear could not keep up.

Lord George Murray's plan was for the leading column to cross the River Nairn two miles from Nairn, march along the east bank for a mile, and then cross back and attack the town. Meanwhile, the column behind would continue along the west bank and finally launch a simultaneous attack on the camp from the west. When the van reached Kilravock, Lord George issued his final orders and Colonel Ker rode off down the column to communicate them to the various leaders so that they could in turn pass them on to their men. The orders said simply that on entering the enemy camp they were not to use their muskets, but having collapsed the tents should strike vigorously with their swords at any bulge in the

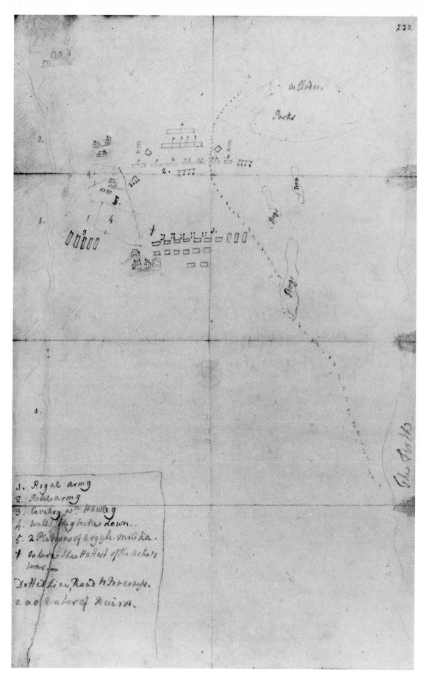

1. Royal army
2. Rebel army
3. Cavalry w.th Hawley
4. wall.t the y broke down.
5. 2 Platoons of argyle militia.
† where the Hottest of the action
   was
X dotted Line Road to Inverness.
o o o water of Nairn.

Rough plan of Culloden by Colonel Joseph Yorke, aide-de-camp to Cumberland and son of the Lord Chancellor, Lord Hardwicke canvas. The Prince sent back by Colonel Ker's hand instructions to Lord George that as the rear was now too far behind to play an immediate part in the attack on the camp, he should fall on it with the men he did have. The timing of the order was awkward for, at the moment of its receipt, Lord George had just emerged from Kilravock wood to find that many of his men had dropped behind during its passage; the path through was so narrow that it was impossible to march abreast, and the weaker had fallen out when there were no comrades alongside to sustain them. He now only had a thousand Highlanders and the gentlemen volunteers of the cavalry who had undertaken to charge with him on foot. Forced to the conclusion that it would be better to call off the night attack, he sent back Cameron of Lochiel to say as much to the Prince.

Charles received the message with the utmost disgust and disappointment; he was particularly upset because it was brought by Lochiel whom he admired. He immediately sent forward the Duke of Perth, Lord John Drummond and Colonel O'Sullivan to investigate the situation. They found Lord George at Knockbuie farm just east of Kilravock Castle. He told them that all the officers up front agreed with his decision to retire as it would soon be daylight and the value of surprise was lost. Colonel O'Sullivan emphasized that it was the Prince's wish for the attack to be carried out, and Lord George replied that he would give the other leaders in the van an opportunity of expressing their views. Most of the officers of Lord Elcho's troops were for carrying on. They had volunteered to take part in the attack because they wished to redeem their poor showing at Falkirk where in their eager charge forward they had nearly lost their horses in a bog. As this had caused ill-natured sneers at their expense, they were determined to be in the thick of the fighting on the present occasion. The gentlemen volunteers, represented by Anderson who had guided the Prince's army through the bog at Prestonpans, Hunter of Burnside and Hepburn of Keith, also all wanted the attack to take place, and were just voicing this opinion when the beat of a drum was heard in the distance.

'Do you hear that?' exclaimed Lord George. 'The enemy are alarmed. We can't surprise them!' 'I never expected to find them asleep,' answered Hepburn, 'but it is much better to march on and attack them than to retreat, for they will certainly follow and oblige us to fight when we shall be in a much worse state than we are now.' 'It is too late,' Lord George replied. 'The day will begin to appear before we could arrive at the camp, and the enemy aware of our approach might take advantage of our situation and attack us while disordered and dispersed.' The volunteers did not agree. They thought the redcoats would be so drunk celebrating Cumberland's birthday that it would make little difference to them whether it were light or not. Hepburn even considered that a little daylight would assist the Highlanders in using their swords. Menzies of Shian, too, wished to go on, and declared, 'If we are to be killed, let it be in plain day, when we can see how our neighbours behave.' But most of the other chiefs agreed with Lord George that to fall upon Cumberland's men in daylight when they were prepared to receive them would be sheer madness. Lochiel justified his *volte-face* by explaining that although he and his brother Dr. Cameron had been as much in favour of the night attack as anybody, they did not now think it feasible because the rear had marched too slowly to be able to join in the fight.

Colonel O'Sullivan now asked if he could speak, but Lord George, thinking he was about to give his personal views, told him rudely they were not of much value as he was an Irish officer in the pay of the French king and likely in the event of a defeat to be treated honourably, and consequently had less to lose than the rest of them. O'Sullivan was obviously deeply hurt, but he merely exclaimed pompously, 'The Prince orders me to tell you that all his confidence is in you. The loss or gain of the Cause is in your hands, and depends entirely upon you. If you march upon the enemy it is morally sure you'll destroy them – having all manner of advantage, surprising them, and the spirits your men are in. You know the situation the Prince is in: neither money nor provisions. If you retire you will discourage your men who suffer enough already. You lose all your advantage and give them over to the enemy.' The only reaction to this came from an officer of the Atholl brigade who asked with a sneer, why those that were so eager did not come and fight with them. To which O'Sullivan retorted, 'I don't know to whom this discourse is addressed. If it be to me you'll know that it was not the first time you saw me in action. You owned yourself, and said it openly, that you saw no other general but the Prince and me at Falkirk. If Lord George will permit me, I'll offer to march in the first rank of the vanguard and will give my head off my shoulders, which is all I have to lose, if he does not succeed. And if he follows I am sure you will follow too, gentlemen.' This pretty speech had no effect on Lord George Murray; but it impressed old Hepburn who drew O'Sullivan aside and begged him to continue pressing the reluctant general. As he left, Hepburn murmured bitterly, 'It was an unhappy day when he joined the Prince; all knew he would ruin the Cause – this is the finishing stroke.'

Just then, the Prince's acting secretary, Hay of Restalrig, rode up and reported, incorrectly as it turned out, that the rear had caught up. When told that a retreat had now been decided on, he went over to Lord George and tried to persuade him to change his mind. He could not turn back without the Prince's permission, Hay said, but Lord George paid no attention. He was convinced that one reason why the march had failed was because Hay had not provided rations for the men: it was

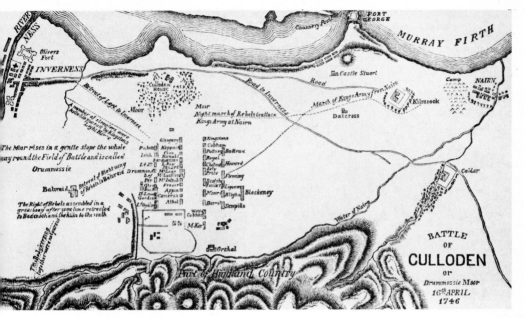

Plan of Culloden, from Home's History

because they were weak from undernourishment that they had dropped out exhausted. Enraged at Lord George's haughty indifference, Hay rode back and warned the Prince that 'unless he came to the front and ordered his Lordship to go on, nothing would be done'. Charles was between the second column and the reserve, which had now lagged so far behind as to form a third column. As he started to ride forward, he met the men from the front of his column coming towards him. 'Where the devil are you going?' he called out. 'We are ordered by the Duke of Perth to return to Culloden House,' he was informed. 'Where is the Duke? Call him here!' the Prince demanded angrily, adding, 'I am betrayed! What need have I to give orders when my orders are disobeyed?'

Wild confusion now reigned as the officers sent to fetch Perth rode up and down each column in turn shouting, 'For God's sake, where is his Lordship?' But, at last, the Duke appeared at the Prince's side. 'What do you mean by ordering the men to turn about?' he was asked. 'Lord George has turned back with the first column three-quarters of an hour ago,' replied Perth. 'Good God! What can be the matter? What does it mean?' expostulated the Prince. 'We are equal in numbers and could have blown them to the devil. Pray, Perth, can't you yet call them back? Perhaps they have not gone too far.' The unhappy Duke, who was devoted to his young master, desperately wanted to help, but did not see how he could. Taking the Prince aside, he was about to explain when Cameron of Lochiel and Colonel O'Sullivan rode up, and Lochiel bluntly did the explaining for him. 'It is now daylight,' he said. 'The project for surprising Cumberland has failed. It is better to turn back than go on and attack when he will be prepared.' Charles was aghast on learning the decision had been taken by Lochiel and others whom he trusted, and he could only blame Lord George for encouraging them to panic. Matters were not helped when O'Sullivan was asked his view and replied emphatically that there would have been ample time to stage an attack. He and some of the other Irish officers, including Brigadier Stapleton and Colonel Ker who had now come up, even suggested that Lord George was betraying them. Although the Prince could not go so far as to believe that, he asked them to keep a close watch on his senior general's future actions. This they willingly agreed to do and, according to Lord Elcho, even promised to shoot him if they found he intended betrayal.

The van, meanwhile, had reached the Inverness road and set off back to Culloden, while the rear had wheeled and followed, not really knowing where it was going. In spite of ever-increasing hunger and weariness the van reached Culloden House in less time than it had taken for the march out. The Prince had intended to go on to Inverness in order to supervise the distribution of the oatmeal stores there, but he was persuaded to leave this task to Fitzjames's horse, and he was back at Culloden House two hours after the van.

Charles felt confident that the royal army would not attack for a day or so, and planned to let his men sleep off their fatigue, besides organizing a supply of oatmeal for them: as the Rev. John Cameron said, 'the Prince intended to give the army a day's rest and a hearty meal'. He also wanted to rest himself but was interrupted by a request from the Marquis d'Eguilles for an audience. As the principal envoy from France, d'Eguilles considered himself responsible for the French element in the Highland army, and in true Gallic fashion pleaded on his knees for Charles to wait before facing a battle with the royal army, because so many of his men were absent, and because those camped around Culloden House were so obviously exhausted. When the Prince showed himself adamant, d'Eguilles departed rapidly for Inverness to burn his official papers, convinced in his own mind that the Prince would lose the coming battle, and concerned for the fate of the Irish picquets, the Ecossais Royaux and the French artillery contingent, who in his view at the very best would soon find themselves prisoners of war.

Because his army had so recently been in contact with Cumberland's men, and there had been no indication that the enemy were about to move, the Prince took few precautions against surprise; so when, only a few hours after his return, news of Cumberland's approach reached Culloden House, confusion reigned supreme. Men staggering with sleep and faint with hunger stood shivering in groups uncertain what to do. Others too exhausted to get up remained lying where they had fallen after the march in sheltered nooks and corners of the moor, many sleeping on in spite of the din of the mustering. Officers galloped hither and thither to carry urgent orders to the different commanders, or to send the cavalry riding down to Inverness to bring back the stragglers. It appeared as if they would never get on the move. But eventually some 5,000 marched out eastwards to take up their positions on the ground selected by Colonel O'Sullivan in his capacity as adjutant and quartermaster general. Because of the urgency of the situation, no attempt was made to reach Lord George's favoured site beyond the Nairn, and the orders of the preceding day were not rewritten though the position chosen was nearer Culloden House. The army no longer had the bog on its left flank, but the right was protected by the walled enclosure of Culwiniac farm as well as by the river. Bearing in mind the shortage of time available the position was probably as good as circumstances could allow.

There was a strong difference of opinion over the value of the enclosures. Colonel O'Sullivan thought they provided useful protection and he had the support of Colonel Ker and Colonel Roy Stewart; but Lord George Murray considered they merely produced a covered approach for the enemy, and he would have made gaps in them to provide fields of fire if he had had time. Close attention was given to how best they might be manned, and the Duke of Perth even came over from the left to voice his opinion. In the end, when Lord George refused to find the necessary men to line the walls, two Gordon regiments[1] were brought up from the second line and placed on either side of the nearest wall.

The Prince directed operations himself, and on his behalf Colonel O'Sullivan set up the army in battle array. However, he was so slow in dealing with the manning of the enclosures on the right that the royal army was almost upon them before he could give his attention to the centre and left. Here, the Macdonalds were causing trouble. Lord George's Athollmen had claimed the coveted position on the right of the line on the previous day, and it should have passed now to the Camerons, but the Camerons conceded it again to the Athollmen. Although the Macdonalds, by an arrangement previously agreed on, were not due for the honour, they considered it their rightful position on all occasions, as it had been since Bannockburn. Disgruntled, they first took up their position in the centre and were with difficulty persuaded to move over to the left, after some of their officers had protested to the Prince.

1. *Avochie's and Stoneywood's.*

'Clanranald, Keppoch and I,' reported Lochgarry, 'begged he would allow us our former right. But he entreated us for his sake we would not dispute it, as he had already agreed to give it to Lord George Murray and his Athollmen. And I have heard that he resented it much, and should never do the like again.'[1] The Duke of Perth under whom the Macdonalds were to serve on the left tried to encourage them by saying that if they behaved with their usual valour, they would make a right out of the left, and he would then change his name to Macdonald; but this did not have much effect. Lord George Murray commanded the right and Lord John Drummond the centre. The Prince at first took up his position behind the second line, but later moved to a hill behind Lord George's men on the right.

Meanwhile, the royal army was advancing slowly in column with the cavalry and the Campbells scouting ahead. When they were two miles from the Highlanders' position, they halted and formed up in lines of battle. It was about eleven o'clock, and it was suggested that the men might be given their dinners before the fight; but Cumberland would have none of it. They would fight better on empty bellies, he said, apart from its being a bad omen – 'remember what a dessert they got to their dinner at Falkirk!' Although the general orders of the day had been read at the head of every regiment before the march began, and each colonel had received instructions in writing, Cumberland now rode along the newly formed lines addressing every battalion; and almost every company. 'Depend, my lads, on your bayonets,' he said. 'Let them mingle with you; let them know the men they have to deal with.' He also delivered a short speech which, although few heard it, was no doubt passed on. He said they were fighting in the best of causes, for their king and country; and he was sure they would win a great victory. If any, however, felt unable to stand firm that day, let them fall out before the battle, for he would rather attack with only one thousand resolute men than ten thousand cowards. Having done his utmost to give his men confidence, Cumberland ordered them to reform into column and continue the approach march; and it was not until they were only a few hundred yards from the Highland army that they were formed into line for the second and last time.

At midday Cumberland and his staff, with only the cavalry and Campbell scouts still ahead on the left, approached the hamlet of Urchal, and near a track junction came upon an enormous boulder which Cumberland mounted and from which he was able to gain a good view of the whole battlefield. Between the enclosures around the farms on his left and the Culloden House enclosures, and beyond some bogs on his right,

1. *Lochgarry's account appears in the Lockhart papers.*

Lord Lothian, an officer on Cumberland's staff at Culloden. By David Morier

he could see the front line of the Highland army stretching nearly a thousand yards across the moor. Noticing some of his guns had stuck in the nearest bog, and the infantry alongside had slung their muskets and were helping to pull them out, he sent instructions to Colonel Belfort to bring his artillery into position in the centre and on the left when the lines were formed, and avoid the soft ground on the right. Having made a mental picture of all that he could see from the top of the boulder, and gratified to notice that his ADC Colonel Joseph Yorke had found time to make two rough maps,[1] he rode off back to the head of his army and from there despatched Lord Bury to make a closer reconnaissance.

Shortly after one o'clock Bury went forward to reconnoitre the position and discover the strength of the Prince's artillery. The latter consisted, he found, of thirteen assorted guns ranging from $1\frac{1}{2}$-pounders to 5-pounders, placed in three batteries on the right, centre and left of the front line, and protected by earth-filled wickerwork gabions. What he did not know, but would have been pleased to learn, was that trained gunners were few: some of these were away in search of food, and the master of the ordnance John Finlayson from Edinburgh had to rely for the most part on unskilled men. The Highlanders were exposed in their long lines to a cold north-east wind which blew in, accompanied by intermittent showers of sleet and snow, from the Moray Firth. They were miserable in their tattered tartans; but the sight of the red-coated officer riding nonchalantly towards them quickly changed their mood. Forgetting their troubles, they were seized with an urge to fight, and gave a great shout and brandished their swords; all of which caused a similar reaction among the redcoats now lined up opposite them, who also immediately started shouting.

Before the noise of their voices died away, the Prince's cannon opened fire, and in a few moments a general bombardment began in which the heavier royal artillery, placed in pairs of guns between the regiments, had the advantage. The royal mortars were brought into action between the first and second lines; and on the river flank, on raised ground short of the first enclosure, a battery was placed to take the Highland lines in enfilade. Owing to the soft ground there was no artillery opposite the Macdonalds on the Highland left, and because of this, and the fact that the opposing lines were farther apart, casualties here at the start of the battle were less heavy than in the Highland centre and right. Cumberland, convinced that the dangerous sector lay towards the Culloden House flank, where he noticed the Macdonalds grudgingly taking up their proper battle positions, promptly not only moved up infantry

1. *One of Yorke's maps is now in the British Museum and the other in the museum on the battlefield.*

reserves and Kingston's volunteer light horse, but took up his own station opposite the Macdonalds.

The Orders of Battle at Culloden

JACOBITE ARMY   HANOVERIAN ARMY

(100?)   *Cavalry*   *(780)*

Lord Balmerino's Life Guards	Lord Cobham's 10th Dragoons
Lord Elcho's Life Guards	(later 10th Hussars)
Fitzjames's Horse, under O'Shea	Lord Mark Kerr's 11th Dragoons
Bagot's Hussars	(later 11th Hussars)
	Duke of Kingston's Light Horse

(?)   *Artillery*   *(120)*

13 guns of various calibres	10 3-pounder battalion guns
	6 coehorn mortars

(4,700)   *Infantry*   *(7,900)*

RIGHT WING

Lord George Murray's Atholl Brigade: (Robertsons, Stewarts, Menzies, Rattrays, Spaldings and Murrays)
    Mercer of Aldie's Athollmen (1st Bn.)
    Menzies of Shian's Athollmen, with Campbells of Glenlyon (3rd Bn.)
    Lord Nairne's Athollmen (2nd Bn.)
Clan Cameron, under Lochiel
Stewarts of Appin, with Maclarens, under Ardsheal
Lovat's Frasers, under Inverallochy

CENTRE

Lady Mackintosh's Clan Chattan, under MacGillivray
Maclachlan's Clan Lachlan, with Macleans under Drimmin, also Raasay Macleods
Farquharsons, under Monaltrie

St. Clair's 1st Foot (Royal Scots)
Howard's 3rd Foot (The Buffs)
Barrell's 4th King's Own Foot (later K.O.R.R.)
Onslow's (or Wolfe's) 8th King's Foot (later King's (Liverpool) Regiment)
Pulteney's 13th Foot (later Somerset Light Infantry)
Price's 14th Foot (later W. Yorks. Regt.)
Bligh's 20th Foot (later Lancs. Fus.)
Campbell's 21st Royal North British Fusiliers (later R.S.F.)
Lord Sempill's 25th Edinburgh Regt. (later K.O.S.B.)
Blakeney's 27th Foot (later Royal Inniskilling Fus.)
Cholmondeley's 34th Foot (later Border Regiment)
Fleming's 36th Foot (later Worcs. Regt.)
Munro's 37th Foot (later R. Hampshire Regiment)

JACOBITE ARMY

John Roy Stewart's Edinburgh Regt.

Chisholms, under the Chief's son

LEFT WING

Clanranald's Macdonalds

Keppoch's Macdonells, with Macdonalds of Glencoe, also some Seaforth Mackenzies under Torridon

Macdonells of Glengarry, under Lochgarry, with Grants of Glen Urquhart

Lord Lewis Gordon's Regiment: Including Stoneywood's Aberdeen Bn. and Avochie's Strathbogie Bn.

Lord Ogilvie's Angus Regt. (2 Bns.)

Bannerman of Elsick's Regiment

Duke of Perth's Regiment with Macgregors

Lord John Drummond's Scots Royal Regiment (in French service)

Lally's, Dillon's and Rooth's Irish Picquets, under Stapleton (in French service)

Gordon of Glenbucket's Regiment

Lord Kilmarnock's Horse Guards

Lord Pitsligo's Banffshire Horse

Lord Strathallan's Perthshire Horse (these three units were dismounted)

HANOVERIAN ARMY

Ligonier's 48th Foot (later Northhants. Regiment)

Battereau's 62nd Foot (later disbanded)

Lord Loudoun's Highlanders (later 64th, then disbanded). One Company only present at the battle

Argyll Militia (Campbells)

Independent Companies, used mostly as baggage guards

It would have been a severe trial for seasoned troops to remain steady under Colonel Belfort's vicious bombardment, and the Highlanders who had not before experienced fire of such intensity 'were greatly surprised and disordered'. Being closer, the Athollmen, Camerons, Appin Stewarts and Frasers of the Highland right were the chief sufferers, and their commanders watched what seemed to be a needless slaughter of their unhappy clansmen with growing impatience. Only too aware

7. CULLODEN.
By David Morier

that his was the weaker side, the Prince planned to wait for the royal army to attack first; but Cumberland was so satisfied with the slaughter caused by his guns that he was content to wait. At last, Cameron of Lochiel sent word to Lord George Murray that he could not hold his men in check any longer. 'They were galled by the enemy's cannon,' he said, 'and were turned so impatient that they were like to break their ranks.' Lord George sent Colonel Ker hurrying off to tell the Prince who immediately ordered the Highland army to attack. But the messengers he dispatched back did not produce a co-ordinated Highland attack as he had hoped. The Mackintoshes in the centre were by now so completely out of Lord Drummond's control that with a wild cry they charged before receiving any orders at all, and were immediately followed by the Macleans and Maclachlans. They had barely started when they were met with a burst of fire from Price's regiment opposite them. This caused them to veer off away from the left and press the clansmen from the right, who had now joined the charge, up against one another so tightly that most of them were quite unable to use their muskets. Only the Macdonalds on the left bided their time.

The combined columns on the right and centre struck mainly Munro's and Barrell's, and as they surged forward were raked by the guns between the regiments, which had changed over to grape, and by the battery on the hill beyond the enclosures. They were also fired at in enfilade by Wolfe's regiment which had been advanced and placed in front of the north wall of the enclosure, and later by Campbells who had broken through the east wall of the enclosure and now lined the north wall beside Wolfe's men. Later still, the Campbells climbed the wall and joined in the hand-to-hand fight. Undaunted, the Highlanders charged, took the two guns ahead of them, and then engaged Sempill's Regiment which was closing the gap behind. There followed a tremendous hand-to-hand struggle between the Highlanders of the right and centre and the men of both lines of the royal army, during which the musket fire of Wolfe's and Sempill's is said to have caused as many casualties among their own men as among the enemy's. General Huske, commanding the second line, noticed this and ordered Sempill's to cease fire. 'Give them the bayonet,' he cried. Lord George Murray had been unhorsed, yet he managed later to go off to bring up his second line; but before these men could arrive, the battle on the Highland right had been fought and lost – by the Highlanders. For once the bayonet, used in the manner in which they had been trained, gained the advantage for the royal soldiers over the Highlanders' broadsword. The Highland right and centre withdrew, not in disorder, but in formed bodies which turned and resisted when pressed; and always well clear of their pursuers who had to be content with despatching the wounded who lay helpless in their path.

On the Highlanders' left, the battle had developed in an altogether different manner. According to Colonel Yorke, the Macdonalds made 'three feints in order to draw our fire', and when these failed, never got to grips as the centre and right had done. The Macdonalds were not at full strength, and some detachments had only joined the army the night before after long forced marches. They also had farther to advance across more difficult ground, and when the Mackintoshes veered off to the right, a great gap was left in the front line which Gordons brought up from the second line, armed solely with muskets, could not adequately fill. Only some small groups led by their gallant chiefs entered into hand-to-hand conflict. Keppoch was one who charged into the midst of the redcoats to meet his death.[1] Macdonald of Scotius rushed forward with twenty followers and died likewise. Clanranald was severely wounded in the desperate fighting. The bulk of the Macdonalds, however, still hung back, not because they refused to charge, but seeing their right flank exposed, and their comrades farther on the right in full retreat, they believed that to close at this time would be useless. Outflanked and out-numbered, the Macdonalds therefore withdrew, a surprising action only in view of their past record.

Meanwhile on the river flank General Hawley's dragoons had passed through the gaps in the walls of the enclosures made for them by the Campbells of the Argyll Militia, and, turning right up the sunken road beyond, were threatening both the Prince on his hill and the flank of the retreating Highlanders. On seeing this new danger, Colonel O'Shea with his sixty troopers of Fitzjames's horse along with Lord Elcho and even fewer of his volunteers, rode forward to hold them back. Neither side charged – the dragoons were too crowded in the lane – but, assisted by the Gordons (Avonche's) from inside the nearest enclosure, the Prince's horsemen held back the 500 royal troopers long enough for the Highlanders to make a relatively orderly withdrawal, and for Charles to escape.

On the left a similar rearguard action was fought to assist the with-drawal of the Macdonalds. Brigadier Stapleton and his Irish picquets, Lally's, Dillon's and Rooth's, came into action and held the pursuing infantry, suffering severe casualties, and Stapleton himself being mortally wounded. The survivors were the last of the Prince's army to leave the battlefield; they marched to Inverness where they surrendered and were accepted as prisoners of war. The Macdonalds were also helped from another direction. Although the Prince's artillery had played a pitifully small part in the battle, one gun detachment now did good work delaying the pursuit of the clansmen. The single gun had arrived too late to join the battery groups, and came into action by the corner of

1. *This spot is now marked by a boulder on the battlefield of Culloden.*

the Culloden House enclosures nearest the battlefield. That its fire
was effective is shown by the fact that four royal 3-pounders and a
mortar were run forward to silence it.[1] But, in spite of this twofold
assistance, the Macdonalds fared worse in their retreat than the rest of
the Highland army. They left the field and made their way to Inverness
in small groups, but were ridden down and slaughtered by Kingston's
bloodthirsty troopers. The Highlanders of the right and centre fared
better. They remained compact enough to deter the dragoons from
attacking, and the latter had to concentrate on despatching individual
stragglers and wounded men, which they did with great brutality,
inspired by their past failures, and encouraged by being told that the
Highlanders themselves would have given no quarter.

Prince Charles himself wanted to stay and rally his men, and was very
reluctant to leave the field, but was finally persuaded to do so by Colonel
O'Sullivan. With a few companions, he rode away to Balvraid, and then
along the east shore of Loch Ness towards Fort Augustus. Meanwhile,
the main body of his army, with losses of a thousand dead, moved off
up the Nairn valley, over Faillie ford and towards Ruthven in Badenoch.
Here, protected by Cluny and his Macphersons who had not managed
to reach Culloden in time to take part in the battle, they consolidated
under Lord George Murray.

*The silver Cumberland Tankard commemorating
the Duke of Cumberland's victory over the
Jacobites at Culloden on April 16, 1746.
By Gabriel Sleath*

1. *The spot is marked by a large stone behind the King's Stables.*

Chapter XI

LONG ISLAND

Sing me a song of a lad that is gone,
Say, could that lad be I?
Merry of soul he sailed on a day
Over the sea to Skye.

ROBERT LOUIS STEVENSON

The Prince was accompanied on the early part of his flight by Colonel O'Sullivan, Sir Thomas Sheridan, Lord Elcho, Captain O'Neil and Sir Alexander Macleod whose servant Ned Burke, a native of South Uist, had been selected as their guide. An early call was at Gortuleg on the south shore of Loch Mhor, and by a strange coincidence Lord Lovat was in residence. He had left Dounie Castle and come to Gortuleg in his territory east of Loch Ness for the sole purpose of avoiding the Prince, and was most embarrassed to have to receive him as his guest. Nevertheless, the cunning and cautious old laird of the Frasers seems to have acted hospitably, and some say he even encouraged the Prince to continue the struggle, reminding him that Robert Bruce had lost eleven battles before winning Scotland in the twelfth. From Gortuleg the Prince sent a letter[1] to Cluny Macpherson at Ruthven saying, 'we have suffered a good deal but hope we shall pay Cumberland in his own coin', and adding that he proposed to review the Frasers, Camerons, Stewarts and Clanranald's and Keppoch's men at Fort Augustus, and hoped Cluny would be able to join and 'bring with you all the people who can possibly be got together'. According to Captain O'Neil, the Prince expected to find the chiefs of the clans already in the neighbourhood of Fort Augustus; but Keppoch was dead, Clanranald badly wounded, and Cameron of Lochiel had had both ankles broken by grapeshot within fifty yards of the guns (when the Camerons were finally driven back, his men paused long enough to lift their beloved chief and carry him off with them in their retreat). Thus, very few of the chiefs, even if they had horses and were still unwounded, could have reached Fort Augustus as quickly as the Prince and his followers.

Finding no one at Fort Augustus, Charles crossed the River Oich and rode down the west shore of Loch Oich to Invergarry Castle. Mac-

---

1. *Written on his behalf by Sir Alexander Macleod.*

130

donell of Glengarry was away – he had gone to Inverness to make his peace with Cumberland, young Angus who had led the Glengarrymen in the Prince's army had been killed at Falkirk, and Invergarry Castle was empty and desolate; there was no food in the larder, the rooms had been emptied of furniture, the place was utterly deserted. Nevertheless, the fugitives did not fare too badly. It was not very comfortable sleeping on the floor, but at daylight Burke spotted a fishing-net stretched across the River Garry, hauled it in, and found two fine salmon, which supplied a good breakfast for the whole party.

At Invergarry, they split up. Only Colonel O'Sullivan, Captain O'Neil and Ned Burke continued with the Prince; the rest went their several ways to try and escape individually. Realizing the clans would not try to reassemble in the neighbourhood, the Prince sent a message by Sir Alexander Macleod to Cluny, and the others at Ruthven: 'Let every man seek his safety in the best way he can.' Chevalier Johnstone, who was at Ruthven, records that, when Macleod arrived and announced the Prince's decision, 'everyone was very sad and despondent at the thought of the plight of their loved ones and their homeland now that their attempt to restore the Stuarts had so obviously failed; and the whole body of assembled Jacobites dispersed, some to skulk in the hills until the hue and cry was over, some to seek a sanctuary in the homes of relatives who were Government supporters, while others hurried away under cover of night to the nearest seaport in the hope of finding a vessel in which to make their escape to France'.

The Prince's little party made their way down the shore of Loch Lochy, and then, turning west past Lochiel's home at Achnacarry, went on along Loch Arkaig to the western end of Glen Pean where they stayed awhile in the hope of receiving information of the whereabouts of the loyal chiefs. When no news arrived, they pressed on across South Morar to a farmhouse by Borrodale near the place where the Prince had first set foot on the mainland of Scotland, and within sight of Loch-nan-Uamh into which the *Du Teillay* had sailed nine months before. Here he was joined by Clanranald, M'Donell of Barrisdale, and John Hay of Restalrig; and by Aeneas Macdonald, whose brother Kinlochmoidart had been captured by Government supporters.

Charles did not feel safe at Borrodale which was in sight of visiting naval vessels, and he planned to try to obtain a boat which could take him to Skye, and to throw himself on the mercy of Sir Alexander Macdonald and Macleod of Macleod. He was now resigned to the fact that he would have to give up his attempt to restore his father to the throne of Britain, and while he waited for a boat, took the opportunity of writing a farewell letter to his chiefs, telling them why he was leaving, and advising them on what they should do; this letter was subsequently sent back to Sir Thomas Sheridan for transmission at a suitable time.

The Prince said that when he came to Scotland 'his only view was to do all in his power for their good and safety', but he saw with grief that at present he could do little for them on this side of the water whereas if he were in France he flattered himself he would be able to persuade the King to give them substantial aid. He suggested that they should meet together to decide how best to defend themselves until French assistance arrived. He said he was sure they could count on support from the Duke of Perth and Lord George Murray. This assumption, however, proved wrong, for the Duke of Perth escaped in a ship to France but died on the way, and Lord George had already sent in his letter of resignation.

Lord George's letter arrived from Ruthven soon after the Prince's message had been despatched to the chiefs, and, surprisingly, it was dated 1 April, 1746, two weeks before the battle of Culloden had been fought. Its contents deeply offended Charles. Lord George said that the Prince should not have embarked on the venture without more positive assurance of substantial French help. He was particularly severe in his criticism of the appointments the Prince had made. In his view, Colonel O'Sullivan had shown himself incapable, and should never have been allowed to continue as adjutant and quartermaster-general; O'Sullivan's main blunder was to refuse to consider a position in the hilly country beyond the Nairn at Culloden; but nothing he had done was right, in Lord George's eyes. He also had much to say concerning Hay of Restalrig's failings. He claimed the disastrous night march to Nairn and the defeat at Culloden had been largely the result of Hay's starving the Prince's army. Lord George ended: 'Your Royal Highness knows I had no design to have continued in the army, even if things had succeeded, gladly would I have laid down by commission, particularly lately when I returned from Atholl, but my friends told me and persuaded me that it would prejudice the Cause at that juncture. I hope your Royal Highness will now accept my demission.' Lord George escaped to Holland, and was later joined by his wife. He remained in exile all his life and attempted on several occasions to see the Prince when they were both living on the Continent; but Charles would never meet him.

While he was waiting near Borrodale, a chance meeting decided the Prince's immediate course of action. During trips across the Minch in search of the gold left by Spanish ships, Aeneas Macdonald had been piloted by an old seaman from Skye named Donald Macleod. The Prince had heard about him from Aeneas, and one day, meeting the man in the woods, Charles asked for his help. Macleod replied that he was getting old and not capable of much, but would certainly do anything he could; on which Charles asked him to take to Sir Alexander Macdonald and the Laird of Macleod on Skye some letters requesting them to shelter him until he could leave for France. Donald Macleod was visibly staggered. He pointed out that the two lairds of his homeland were the Prince's enemies, and were even then searching for him, their militia combing the hills no farther away than ten or twelve miles across the sea. The sooner he left Borrodale the better, for at any moment they might put to sea and carry their search to the mainland. Macleod then suggested that he might be allowed to hire a boat and engage a crew to take the Prince to some hiding place in the Outer Hebrides out of reach of the navy and militia. When Charles consulted his friends, Clanranald and Barrisdale were not convinced that it was wise for the Prince to move away from Borrodale; but Colonel O'Sullivan agreed with the old boatman, and persuaded Charles to go, suggesting as a refuge the island of Benbecula[1] which belonged to Clanranald's father, old Clanranald of South Uist, whom they had contacted and found mildly sympathetic nine months before on their arrival at Eriskay in the *Du Teillay*.

The Prince acquired an eight-oared boat with a loose-footed square sail on a yard from Angus Macdonald of Borrodale House, and accompanied by Colonel O'Sullivan, Father Allan Macdonald, Captain O'Neil, and his guide and servant Ned Burke, he put himself in the care of Donald Macleod and his crew. It was a rough passage, at one time so rough that it was feared they might be cast up on the shores of Skye and fall prey to a prowling militia company. There was talk of turning back, but Donald Macleod thought it safer in the open sea than among the rocks of the mainland; he kept straight ahead, and by his good seamanship eventually landed them in a creek near Rossinish on the north-east coast of Benbecula where they found sanctuary in a deserted shieling (or fisherman's hut) near the shore.

Old Clanranald, who lived at Nunton seven miles away on the west coast of the island, heard of the arrival of the strangers and although hardly an enthusiastic supporter of the Prince went over to see them. With his approval they decided to pose as merchants from Orkney who had been shipwrecked and were now on their way in a small boat to Stornoway to buy a serviceable merchantman to carry on their business. They later left Benbecula for Stornoway, and arrived there on 5 May having called at Scalpa en route. They covered the last ten miles across Lewis from Loch Seaforth on foot. The country was extremely rough, consisting of trackless moors cut up by lochs and rivers; and they waded through streams, stumbled over peat-hags and boulders, and struggled through bogs for hours on end, reaching Arnish two miles from Stornoway in a thoroughly exhausted condition. At Arnish, however, they were received hospitably by Mrs. Mackenzie of Kildare and soon recovered.

1. Some say the destination was Eriskay.

Donald Macleod had gone ahead of the land party by boat to Stornoway to buy the larger vessel required. At first he had some success, and managed to acquire the option of a merchantman; but later, when news reached Stornoway of who the purchaser really was, not only was the deal cancelled, but Donald Macleod learnt that a Mackenzie militia company was being mustered to apprehend the Prince. Just in time, he brought the small boat across the harbour, got the Prince and his followers aboard, and headed back again for Benbecula. In order to evade the naval vessels searching the waters, they hugged the coasts, but while skirting the shores of Lewis, were followed by four sloops, and had to put into Loch Shell to escape them. They landed on an island in the mouth of the Loch and spent three days in empty fishing huts living off the fish laid out to dry on the sloping rocks. When they continued to Scalpa, they again saw warships in pursuit and were forced to enter Loch Tarbert and sail right round Scalpa to avoid them. Having skilfully escaped from yet more enemy craft off the Harris sound, they eventually landed on an island in an arm of the sea off the east coast of Benbecula just south of Rossinish, and occupied what Ned Burke called 'a grasskeeper's bothy'.

As rain was falling in torrents, they were very glad to get under cover. A strong wind was blowing offshore, and as this was likely to drive off the threatening warships, the sound of it roaring round the cabin made them feel more secure. A messenger was quickly sent across the island to Nunton to warn old Clanranald of their arrival, and on the next day he paid them a visit, bringing with him his family's tutor and local schoolmaster Neil McEachain who the chief said would conduct them to a sanctuary in the south where they would be quite safe from both militia companies and naval vessels. On the night of 14 May, Charles and his small party were led fifteen miles across Benbecula and South Uist to Glen Corodale which lies between Mount Hekla and Ben More, the two highest mountains in South Uist. In the glen there were two forester's cottages which provided comfortable quarters for the Prince and his followers during the three weeks they spent there. Under the protection of old Clanranald and his people the Prince felt more secure than he had done at any time since his flight from Culloden. He was also made very comfortable. Kegs of brandy – his favourite drink – were brought to him, and he was able to carouse with local friends like Macdonald of Boisdale. Boisdale's wife, meanwhile, kept him well supplied with reading matter and other comforts.

On 23 May, while the Prince was at Corodale, his cousin the Duke of Cumberland left Inverness and moved to Fort Augustus where he established his headquarters until 18 July when he handed over command to Lord Albemarle and General John Campbell of Mamore and returned to England. He had successfully completed the first part of his task, that of active military operations; he had also arranged the disposal of prisoners and booty, and was now ready for the next phase which was, as he wrote to the Prime Minister, 'to destroy utterly the spirit of rebellion in the Highlands'. To carry out this policy, he considered it necessary to harry the glens, and to burn down the homes of the Jacobite chiefs and the houses of their clansmen. The Grants of Glenmoriston, which lay conveniently near Fort Augustus, were the first to feel the impact. The whole glen was stripped and burnt by Cholmondeley's regiment (34th) and Macleod militiamen from Skye. Wide paths of destruction were created in the glens of the Camerons, Macdonalds, Frasers and Macphersons, and before Cumberland left Scotland, Lochiel's Achnacarry home, Glengarry's Invergarry castle, Lovat's castle at Dounie, and Cluny's castle, as well as countless houses of lesser lairds and tacksmen, had been put to the torch.

Among the most vigorous in this harassment of the rebels were two Scots, Captain Fergussone of the *Furnace* and Captain Caroline Scott of Guise's. Fergussone was serving in Captain Noel's squadron, whose main duties were to police the Minch, to try to intercept Spanish and French ships, and to endeavour to capture the Prince. For the last task, Fergussone transported troops from island to island so that they could search for Charles; but he also took part in burning the homes and staving in the boats of the rebels. As early as March 1746 he is recorded, together with a fellow naval captain and east-country Scot named Duff, as burning townships along the Morven shore in the Sound of Mull. He worked in co-operation with the soldiers of Captain Scott's regiment, ferrying them along the channels of the western isles so that they could carry out their searches, interrogations and destruction. After his victory at Culloden, Cumberland had released the men of Guise's Regiment who had been taken prisoner by the Jacobites at the surrender of Inverness Castle, and sent them back to Berwick; but, although he intended to relieve also the remnant of the regiment at Fort William, in the end he employed the heroes of the siege – Captain Scott and his men – in hunting the fugitives. From the Duke's point of view this was a wise decision. Scott was more ruthless than the kindly old General John Campbell of Mamore, and became a terror to the rebels; even his own brother officers became disgusted at his brutality and 'expostulated with him, begging him to consider what he was doing'.

In June the Prince's friends came to the conclusion that it was no longer safe for him to remain at Corodale. A company of Skye militiamen commanded by Captain Hugh Macdonald was reported to be on the way from Barra to South Uist; *H.M.S. Furnace*, under the dreaded Captain Fergussone, was known to be cruising in the vicinity; and the channel between Long Island and Skye was said to be crammed with Government vessels. Charles, therefore, resumed his travels. First he went north by boat and lived in a cave on an island off Benbecula. Then, after only two days, he was ferried back and walked with Captain O'Neil and Ned Burke to his earlier refuge-place near Rossinish. According to Ned Burke they stayed at Rossinish for a few days 'but the enemy came to that country likewise in search of the Prince'. Before they left Lady Clanranald, who was more sympathetic than her husband, travelled the five miles from Nunton and brought the Prince a supply of foodstuffs and other comforts with which he said he was so delighted that 'he would never forget how kind she had been'.

With enemy ships cruising nearby, it was difficult to get away from Rossinish; but eventually under cover of darkness the Prince was taken off by boat back towards Corodale. As no less than fifteen sails could be seen off Corodale, they continued south, hugging the coast, put into the wide estuary of Loch Boisdale, and established themselves in a ruined castle on an island. But Captain Scott and his men had landed within a mile of them, so they rowed over to the mainland and took refuge in the hills. When they thought the coast was clear, a messenger was sent to Macdonald of Boisdale's home nearby, but to their great disappointment he returned with the news that Boisdale had been taken away as a prisoner by Scott. His wife, however, sent them some welcome bottles of brandy and some bread and cheese.

At the instigation of Captain O'Neil, the Prince's friends now began to plan to remove him from the dangers of Long Island over to Skye where he might be safer. Both Lady Clanranald and the mother of Flora Macdonald became involved in the project, and through them Flora herself. Flora Macdonald was descended from the ancient line of the Clanranald chiefs and was treated by old Clanranald as one of the family on her frequent visits to Nunton. Aged twenty-four, she was well educated and had mixed in Society in Edinburgh under the chaperonage of her kinswoman the Countess of Eglinton. Her father had died and her mother married for the second time Hugh Macdonald of Armadale in Skye, the militia captain ironically enough engaged in searching for Prince Charles. Though on good terms with her stepfather in Skye, Flora had remained in South Uist, and she kept house for her brother at Milton on the west coast of the island. Flora heard about the Prince's presence among them during her visits to Nunton. Another frequent visitor was Captain O'Neil, while acting as go-between for Lady Clanranald and the Prince. He soon became greatly attracted to Flora, and noticing the obvious interest she displayed in the Prince and the sympathy she expressed for him in his plight, decided to try to involve her in his scheme to spirit the Prince away to Skye, in the planning of which, unknown to Flora, her stepfather played a part. The idea was for her stepfather, because of the dangerous situation in Long Island, to send her back to Skye in the company of a man-servant and a maid – and the latter was to be the Prince in disguise. The plan involved only Neil McEachain, who as a Gaelic speaker was chosen as the manservant, so the disappointed and lovesick O'Neil would be forced to watch his rival depart with his beloved Flora while he remained behind to seek his own means of escape; but O'Neil loyally accepted this.

Before the Prince left Boisdale on the start of his new venture, he said good-bye to three friends who had looked after him faithfully during his travels: Colonel O'Sullivan, who had been his staunch companion from the very beginning, Donald Macleod who had piloted him to Long Island, and Ned Burke who had been his guide and servant ever since Culloden. O'Sullivan and Burke later managed to escape; but Donald Macleod was captured by the militia. When he was examined by General Campbell, the latter tried to explain to him how easily he might have gained the Government reward of £30,000 and how such a sum would have made him and his family happy for ever. 'What then,' exclaimed the staunch old Highlander, '£30,000! Though I had gotten it I could not have enjoyed it eighty-four hours. Conscience would have gotten up upon me. That money could not have kept it down. And tho' I could have gotten all England and Scotland for my pains I would not have allowed a hair of his body to be touched if I could help it.'

In order to persuade Flora Macdonald to go to Skye, Captain O'Neil arranged for the Prince to meet her in a secluded shieling near her home at Milton, a few miles to the north-west of Loch Boisdale. Leaving the others on the shore of the Loch, and guided by Neil McEachain, the Prince and O'Neil trudged across the moor to Milton. O'Neil had warned Flora that he was bringing a friend, and she probably knew to whom he was referring. When they had knocked on the door of the shieling, and been shown into her room, she received them with the utmost courtesy, and offered them refreshments of oatcakes, milk and cream. O'Neil explained the plan. He said it would be quite simple, as her stepfather would provide the necessary passes so that they could get through the cordons of militiamen and naval vessels abounding in the neighbourhood of Long Island. Unexpectedly, Flora declined. She pointed out that her stepfather was an officer of the militia, and she would be asking him to neglect his duty; also that her kinswoman Lady Margaret Macdonald – who they expected to receive them at Kilbride in Skye – was the wife of Sir Alexander Macdonald of Sleat, an avowed Government supporter. If she took the Prince to them, as was suggested, she would ruin him and his wife. Captain O'Neil did all in his power to make her change her mind. He said that Sir Alexander was at Fort William with the Duke of Cumberland and therefore could not be accused of connivance, and that her mother's house was near Kilbride and the Prince could easily and quickly be conducted there. When O'Neil seemed to be making no headway the Prince himself took a hand. Instead of explaining how easy it was, as O'Neil had tried to do, he stressed rather the dangers, and the satisfaction that would come from over-coming them. Using all his light-hearted charm he showed it as a thrilling adventure which she would remember with pride to the end of her days. This was too much for the susceptible young woman. Who could resist darling handsome Prince Charles in such a mood? She agreed to ride up to Nunton and consult with Lady Clanranald. She said she would let them know her decision within a few hours.

The Prince and his two companions made off in a north-easterly direction towards the slopes of Mount Hekla to wait in a shelter among the rocks for Flora Macdonald's reply. So far all had gone well, but now their troubles were to begin. The water between South Uist and Ben-becula could be crossed by a ford, but when Flora reached it on her way from Milton to Nunton she found it guarded by militiamen who stopped and detained her. When by the afternoon of the next day the Prince had still not heard from her, he sent Neil McEachain to Nunton to investi-gate; but he also was arrested at the same ford. Then at last their luck turned. Flora's stepfather arrived at the ford, and Flora and Neil were both released. The Prince was told by the returning schoolmaster that Flora had decided to help and the plan was for him to start his journey to Skye from Rossinish; so they set out to reach it again as best they could, no mean task through country swarming with militia, and across waters patrolled by the navy.

Travelling by night, partly on foot and partly by boat, they landed eventually on an island in Loch Uskavagh; and much to the Prince's annoyance had to wait several hours for the tide to turn before they could wade ashore and make for Rossinish. There they found a rough and ready lodging in a bothy on the shore, but spent a by no means carefree time there. Militiamen nearby collected milk daily from the bothy, and when they were about, the Prince and his two friends had to rush off down to the beach and hide among the rocks. Then, after Lady Clan-ranald and Flora Macdonald had arranged to come and see them, a report that twenty militiamen had arrived at Nunton sent them scurry-ing back. General John Campbell with 1,500 men were later rumoured to have landed not far from Nunton, and Captain Fergussone with an advance party was said to be already in residence; but this was after all the preparations had been completed. During a period when the milk-collecting militiamen had left the vicinity, Lady Clanranald and Flora came over from Nunton with Charles's clothes. The good-looking Prince seems to have made an attractive 'Betty Burke', to judge from his picture. According to Neil McEachain, when everyone who was not to

Charles as Betty Burke by J. Williams

accompany him to Skye had departed, Flora asked him demurely to dress himself, and 'the Prince stripped off his own clothes (except, it seems, for his breeches) and was dressed by Miss Flora, in his new attire, but could not keep his hands from adjusting his headdress which he cursed a thousand times. The gown was of calico with a light coloured quilted petticoat, and the mantle was of dull camlet made after the Irish fashion'. He wanted to carry a pistol under his petticoat; but Flora objected, saying that, if he were searched, it would give him away. To which he replied a shade coarsely, 'Indeed, Miss, if we shall happen with any that will go so narrowly to work in searching, they will certainly discover me at any rate.'

The boat provided by Lady Clanranald was an eighteen-footer with oars and sail. On 28 June, they rowed across to Arasay and waited on a rainy evening for the protection of night. There was a final alarm when four wherries with armed men aboard sailed into Loch Uskavagh; but the vessels passed without stopping to search the shore, and as soon as it became dark, they set off. There was no wind, and for some hours they hugged the shore of North Uist. Only when they reached Loch Maddy did they turn east towards Skye. At midnight it started to blow from the west with rain in the wind, and the sea became rough. This worsening in the weather, however, seemed only to raise the already high spirits of the Prince, and, according to Flora, 'he began to sing to entertain the company'. During the last hours of the night, worn out by strain and excitement, Flora lay asleep in the bottom boards of the boat with the Prince sitting beside her awake and alert, and protecting her with his arm from the crew when they stumbled forward to trim the sail. At dawn it was still again, and misty; then suddenly it cleared and the coast of Skye was seen. There was now not wind enough to use the sail, so they rowed round the western point of Loch Snizort. On the far side, two Macleod militia sentries spotted them and told them to pull in, and one of the men ran to call out the guard while the other pointed his musket; but it misfired. When the platoon assembled, it looked as if they were about to fire a volley, but the men changed their minds and let the boat pull away unmolested. They were soon across the bay and landed in a little creek just to the north of Kilbride within a short distance of the home of Lady Margaret Macdonald.

Leaving Prince Charles to wait impatiently in the boat, Flora accompanied by Neil McEachain set out to inform Lady Margaret of their arrival. On the way she met one of Lady Margaret's servants who confirmed that Sir Alexander was away at Fort Augustus, but said that the officer commanding the local Macleod militia, Sir Alexander's factor and some local ladies were with her ladyship. The presence of the militia officer in the house at such a time was most disturbing. Lady Margaret, however, managed to enlist the help of her husband's factor, and persuaded him to take the Prince to the comparative safety of his own home seven miles to the south on the way to Portree. She also left Flora to convince the militia officer of the innocent purpose of the party which had just arrived. Flora was helped in the deception by being able to show an unsealed letter given her by her stepfather before she set out.

It was written to his wife and read as follows:

'My dear Marion – I have sent your daughter from this country lest she should be in any way frightened by the troops lying here. She has got one Betty Burke, an Irish girl, who, as he tells me, is a good spinster. If her spinning pleases, you can keep her until she spins all your lint; or if you have any wool to spin, you may employ her. I have sent Neil McEachain along with your daughter, and Betty Burke to take care of them – I am, your dutiful husband – Hugh Macdonald.
22 June, 1746.'

When the militia officer saw Flora's stepfather's name on the letter he appeared quite reassured; he did not even consider it necessary to search the boat.

The Prince thoroughly enjoyed his night in the factor's house. After a splendid supper, at which Flora sat on his right hand and the factor's wife on his left, the factor produced a bowl of hot punch and the two men had a long evening's carouse; after which the Prince slept well, and late. Next morning, the ladies went to Charles's room to dress him up again in his female attire. They took this precaution in order to deceive the servants and neighbours who had already become suspicious – one even had been heard to say, 'Bless me, what long strides the jade takes, and how awkwardly she manages her petticoats.' Before Flora put on Charles's headdress, the factor's wife asked her in Gaelic to try to persuade him to give them a lock of his hair. Flora refused, and told her to ask him herself. Charles, who could not understand what they were saying, enquired what was the matter. When they told him, he knelt down, put his head on Flora's lap, and told her to cut off a lock. This they divided, blushing with pleasure and embarrassment. The factor now appeared and, seeing that the Prince's shoes were worn out, offered him a new pair of his own. Taking the discarded pair in exchange, he exclaimed, 'I will faithfully keep these shoes until you are safely in St. James's when I will come and see you and show them you to put you in mind of your night's entertainment and protection under my roof.' All of which greatly pleased the Prince; and he came to the conclusion that the factor was the pleasantest person he had encountered, although the servant of a Government supporter.

Charles was taken by a guide to Portree, and in a wood on the way divested himself of his female attire; 'Betty Burke' was no more. Both Neil McEachain and Flora Macdonald joined him at Portree; but neither they nor the Prince were to remain very long, for it was planned that he should be taken to the off-shore island of Raasay and placed under the protection of the young laird. Although Raasay had been ravaged by Government forces, these had now departed and the laird was known to be a most loyal supporter of the Prince.

Flora Macdonald by Allan Ramsay

It was in a room at the inn at Portree, where the Prince's friends assembled, that this most dramatic episode in his adventure came to an end, and he said good-bye to Flora Macdonald. Remembering a small debt, he gave her the half crown she had lent him when her servant; he presented her with his own miniature portrait; and he exclaimed, 'For all that has happened, I hope, Madam, we shall meet in St. James's yet.' Then he left the brave woman to whom he owed so much, and was rowed across to Raasay. They were never to meet again.

8. FLORA MACDONALD.
By Richard Wilson

9. THE ISLAND OF SKYE.

Chapter XII

LOCH-NAN-UAMH

'The gentlemen of Clanranald had been responsible for the Prince's safety, and they knew how to find him.'
JOHN S. GIBSON'S Ships of the '45

After the Prince had departed for Benbecula, a few of his chiefs met in the neighbourhood of Loch-nan-Uamh to co-ordinate plans for further resistance. When on 30 April, 1746, two French 36-gun privateers sailed into the Loch, and the news of their arrival spread throughout the neighbouring countryside, other Jacobite leaders[1] appeared, some with the intention of escaping to France. Meetings were held at which were present the wounded Cameron of Lochiel, young Clanranald, Lord Lovat, M'Donell of Barrisdale and the invalid Murray of Broughton who had made the journey with great difficulty. The chiefs pledged themselves to go on fighting, and as the ships had brought not only weapons and ammunition but also gold, Murray of Broughton decided that, while most of the barrels of money should be buried in a secret place in the woods to await the Prince's instructions for disposal, some gold should be immediately distributed to the chiefs to help them continue the struggle.

When they heard that Prince Charles was nowhere at hand, the captains of the *Mars* and the *Bellone* were not disposed to allow the gold to be landed. But the arrival in the loch of Captain Thomas Noel in the 24-gun *Greyhound* accompanied by two smaller vessels caused the French captains to change their minds. They quickly landed their weapons, and barrels of brandy, powder and gold, and then turned to meet the intruders. They were not unduly alarmed, for they felt that their 36-gun ships with full complements of soldiers were more than a match for their opponents.

The policing of the seas around Scotland was in the hands of Commodore Thomas Smith, later Rear Admiral of the Red; but Smith confined his activities largely to the east coast, and only occasionally sailed round Cape Wrath into the Minch. The seas, lochs and channels of the western coasts and islands were, therefore, the responsibility of Captains

---

1. *Sir Thomas Sheridan, the Duke of Perth and Lord John Drummond, Lord Elcho and John Hay.*

143

Noel, Fergussone and Duff, with Noel as senior captain in overall command when they came together.

The battle in Loch-nan-Uamh between Captain Noel's three vessels and the French ships proved to be a fierce one; and as it was watched by numerous Highlanders from the shore, and written up in the ships' logs, it has been fully recorded. The French ships were prepared for action, and when the British vessels were clearly seen, the French colours were hoisted and all made ready. The *Bellone* was under-way before the British approached, but the *Mars* was still at anchor; and it was towards the latter ship which the *Greyhound* sailed, delivering a broadside which smashed mountings and swept the deck, killing seventeen soldiers including a refugee officer of the Régiment Royal Ecossais who had insisted on taking part in the battle. Being at anchor, the *Mars* could only reply with her forecastle guns, and suffered more damage than her small opponent. Captain Noel now sailed off to give the *Bellone* as many of his guns as could be reloaded; but this time he did not have a similar success. The *Bellone* manoeuvred and exchanged broadsides, with the advantage going to the larger ship. According to Noel, the

Commodore Smith, who commanded the naval forces guarding Scotland but directed most of his attention to the east coast. After R. Wilson

Greyhound suffered badly, and 'her fore-topsail ties and most of her braes' were shot away. The *Bellone* steered to windward of *Greyhound* with the intention of boarding her, but there was not a fair breeze and she turned instead and drew up to protect her sister ship; they both then lay off the bay where the arms and gold had been landed earlier. Now the smaller British vessels attacked, sailing up and delivering their broadsides at the *Bellone*, but not coming within musket range. Then the *Greyhound* came in again. The *Bellone* replied at once to every volley she received, and each time got the better of the exchange so that at last the crippled British ships drew off, yards shot away and shrouds cut to ribbons. Before *Greyhound* left the loch she was able to turn her guns on the Highlanders who were busy on shore carrying away what had been landed from the French ships. Then, after six hours of fighting, the battle of Loch-nan-Uamh came to an end.

Throughout that long evening of early summer, every effort was made aboard the French ships to get ready to sail; while on shore it was the brandy which received the most attention. Heavy drinking began before nightfall; and, in the resulting disorder, Barrisdale's and Fraser's men were able to make off with a great deal more than their share of the gold which Murray of Broughton had agreed should be distributed.

The *Mars* and the *Bellone* sailed next morning. They carried with them the Duke of Perth, who died before reaching France, his brother

The Battle of Loch-nan-Uamh: The Greyhound *leads the* Baltimore *and the* Terror *against* La Bellone. *By Charles Brooking*

Lord John Drummond, Lord Elcho, Sir Thomas Sheridan, Lockhart and John Hay.

Charles did not linger on Raasay. Although the laird was anxious to give him refuge, the island could not offer the hiding place the Prince was seeking. So he returned the following day to Skye, ostensibly to discover at first hand how matters stood, but in reality to slip away. Without prior announcement to his host, on the grounds of secrecy, he made off on foot accompanied only by Captain Malcolm Macleod to seek asylum with the Mackinnons in the vicinity of Ellagol in the south of the island. The Mackinnons welcomed the Prince hospitably; but the hiding places they could offer were not considered safe either, so they rowed him round the point of Sleat to Loch Nevis on the mainland with the intention of putting him in the safe-keeping of Macdonald of Morar.

While Charles was at Loch Nevis he was very nearly captured. The militia were known to be in the neighbourhood so, after the Prince's party had landed, he and young Mackinnon remained in hiding near the shore for three days while old Mackinnon set out on foot to see how the land lay. When they did get moving once again, and were passing round a promontory, they came unexpectedly on an empty tied-up militia boat, and went so close that they struck it with one of their oars. The militiamen, easily recognizable by the red cross on their bonnets, were standing talking not far away, and they hailed the Prince's party and asked them where they came from. The Prince's boatman replied that they had come from Sleat. They were ordered to come ashore. But instead of doing so, they steered towards the centre of the loch, rowing away as fast as they could; on which the militiamen jumped into their boat and gave chase. When it was thought that the pursuers might catch them up, John Mackinnon ordered the boatmen to load their muskets. He told them that if it came to a fight they must try and kill all the men coming after them so that no one should learn what had happened. Charles, who lay concealed at the bottom of the boat with Mackinnon's plaid spread over him, asked from time to time how they were getting on, and was reassured by being told, first that they were holding their own, and later that they were outdistancing their pursuers. When the militia boat was almost out of sight, the Prince's party made for a wood which came down to the water's edge on the far shore, and jumping out dashed in and hid themselves in the thickets, pulling the boat after them. Later, when they emerged on the far side of the wood well up the hill slope, they noticed with satisfaction that their pursuers had given up the chase and were rowing disconsolately away.

It had been reported that both old Clanranald and his son were staying nearby, but only the old chief could be found. The Mackinnons asked him to provide a refuge for the Prince, but Clanranald, remembering the trouble the Prince's presence had caused on Benbecula, refused to involve himself further. And they met with an equally cold reception from Macdonald of Morar when they moved to South Morar. This second unexpected refusal to help almost reduced Charles to despair. He is said to have cried out: 'Oh, God Almighty! Look down upon my circumstances and pity me in my most melancholy situation, for some of those who joined me at first, and appeared to be fast friends now turn their backs upon me in my greatest need.' Addressing Mackinnon, the Prince said, 'I hope you will not desert me too.' To which the old laird replied with tears in his eyes, 'I will never leave your highness in the day of danger, but will go with you wherever you order me.' Charles then asked to be taken to Angus Macdonald of Borrodale who was rumoured to be hiding in a hut in the woods near Loch-nan-Uamh. Borrodale, who had been helpful at the start of the venture, and also when the Prince left for Benbecula, once again did all in his power to assist. Judging his own hut insufficiently secure, he led the Prince to an almost inaccessible cave four miles away, and this became Charles's home for a time.

The unpleasant discovery was now made that they were surrounded by Government forces: a chain of militia posts stretched across the heads of Loch Nevis, Loch More and Loch Shiel, and naval vessels guarded the lochs' mouths. In view of this situation, it was decided to try and break through the land cordon and take the Prince away to Mackenzie territory to the west of Inverness; as the Mackenzies had not come out in support of the Prince, not only had their country not been despoiled, but it was likely to be free from search parties.

Charles was skilfully led through the militia posts by Macdonald of Glenaladale and Borrodale's son, and managed to avoid contact in spite of passing close by the enemy on several occasions. In the neighbourhood of Loch Arkaig, they were joined by Dr. Cameron who was familiar with the country and led them first past the battlefield of Glenshiel, and then through Chisholm and Fraser country to Strath Glass, twenty miles west of Inverness. Here the Prince was again accommodated in a cave, and joined later by young Clanranald. The young laird proved much more sympathetic than his father had been. Hearing they were short of food, he immediately offered to go and forage for some, 'at the point of the sword, if necessary'.

While the Prince was at Strath Glass, the search for him slackened as a result of the gallant action of Roderick Mackenzie, who, although his clan was not involved, had become one of the Prince's lifeguards. Mackenzie was the same age as the Prince and resembled him closely in looks. While skulking in the hills near Glenshiel, he was surprised by a party of Captain Caroline Scott's soldiers. Mackenzie tried to escape but, being overtaken, drew his sword and defended himself. One of the soldiers raised his musket and shot him, and as he fell he cried out just before he died, 'You have killed your Prince! You have killed your Prince!' Mackenzie looked so like Charles that the soldiers believed they really had killed the young Prince. They cut off his head and took it back with them to Fort Augustus, and it was some time before it was realized that they had made a mistake.

Less satisfaction was derived from the news that reached them of double-dealing by M'Donell of Barrisdale. Coll M'Donell the younger had earlier joined the Prince; but he had not been present at Culloden as he had been sent north to try and retrieve the gold brought by the *Prince Charles*. Before the uprising he was notable as one of the leading cattle stealers in the Highlands, and also the foremost exponent of the Scottish practice which added a new word to the English language. This was black-meal, or blackmail, a forced levy in meal which, if produced by chiefs, would ensure that their cattle would be protected by Barrisdale's men from lesser thieves. By collecting these impositions, Barrisdale became wealthy enough to build himself one of the finest houses in the Highlands on a splendid site with views across Loch Hourne, and with 'eighteen firerooms and many others without fires, and beautifully covered with blue slates'. Barrisdale had played a double game before. When the Frasers planned to capture Duncan Forbes at Culloden House, he had sent a warning to the Lord President. It was now learnt that, after Barrisdale had been taken prisoner, he had been released from Fort Augustus on undertaking to help the authorities; and although his co-operation with the Government did not stop Captain Fergussone from turning the guns of his frigate on his fine house, it did at least result in his cattle being spared. It was heard, too, that Barrisdale had agreed to advise on the best way of cordoning off the country and capturing the Prince, and it was decided that in the interests of security the Prince must go on his travels again.

The only Highlanders still under arms were the Camerons under Cameron of Clunes who were guarding the wounded Lochiel in his hide-out in the woods near Achnacarry to the west of Loch Lochy, and the Macphersons protecting Cluny in one or other of his hiding places in Badenoch or on the slopes of Ben Alder twenty miles east of Ben Nevis. With this knowledge in mind, it was decided that the best course was to put the Prince in the care of these two lairds.

While he was in his first new refuge with Cameron of Clunes, the Prince expressed a wish to see his old friend Lochiel. At first Clunes demurred, saying it was too dangerous with so many militia search parties scouring the countryside. Later, however, Charles was taken to see the laird – and was nearly shot by Lochiel's guards for his pains. Fortunately he was recognized just before they opened fire. On seeing the Prince approaching his hut, Lochiel hobbled out to meet him. He was about to kneel, but the Prince stopped him. Putting his hand affectionately on Lochiel's shoulder, he said, 'Oh no, my dear Lochiel. We do not know who may be watching from the top of the hills over there, and if they see any such motion they will immediately conclude that I am here.' When he entered the hut, the Prince was amazed to find it stocked with food of all descriptions: joints of mutton, ham, bacon, sausages, butter and cheese, and whisky galore. Lochiel prepared a splendid meal and, when it was finished, Charles exclaimed, 'Now, gentlemen, I really have eaten like a prince.' While he was with the Camerons, the Prince was visited by Chevalier Lancize who had come from France and landed in search for him. The Chevalier had arrived in a vessel manned by the Maurepas contingent which had turned back on the disabled *Elisabeth* at the very start of the venture. Except for Lancize and a companion who reached the Prince, they were even more unlucky on their second attempt, for their new ship was captured by the British navy in Loch Broom on the west coast.

From Cameron country the Prince was taken to be placed in the care of the Macphersons. There was some difficulty in discovering where Cluny was; but eventually he was traced to a hiding place on Ben Alder known as 'The Cage'. 'The Cage' had been constructed in a wood high up on the slopes of the mountain. The floor was formed from logs laid on end, raised on the downhill side to make a level platform. Trees already growing on the hillside were trimmed to provide the uprights, and the sides and roof were constructed of interwoven boughs and heather. A large fallen tree which lay naturally across the top gave the refuge its name. Accommodating seven people comfortably, it provided a secure home for the Prince and his companions until the fortunate day when he at last heard that a ship had arrived from France to take him away.

The first attempts to rescue the Prince were made at the instigation of Antoine Walsh. Following the *Mars* and the *Bellone*, a small ship was sent which managed to put in at Loch-nan-Uamh, but achieved nothing. A further attempt was more successful, for at least the vessel took off Colonel O'Sullivan. She also got news of the Prince's whereabouts, and her captain waited for a time while O'Neil tried to find him; but, in the end, threatened with capture by British warships, she made off without either the Prince or O'Neil. The next ship that set out on the same errand was the one manned by the Maurepas contingent, which was captured in Loch Broom. Until the disaster at Culloden, and the ending of all the Prince's hopes, the French minister for the navy and the authorities in general had been enthusiastic supporters of Antoine Walsh in his efforts on behalf of the Prince; but when they realized that Charles had failed, Walsh was discredited and he drops out of the picture. Fortunately, another loyal supporter of the Prince was available in France to take over the organization of the rescue attempts. He was the young Irishman, Captain Warren. Warren had been sent back from Scotland after the satisfactory conclusion of the northern campaign against Loudoun and Macleod, as it was hoped that the news of this success on the part of the Prince's forces would produce increased help from the French king, particularly if it were brought personally by an enthusiast for the Cause such as Warren. Reports of the disaster at Culloden ruined any advantageous effects the earlier victories might have produced; but this did not deter Warren from setting about organizing a well planned relief attempt. When Antoine Walsh told him that there were no suitable ships at Nantes except the *Mars* and the *Bellone*, which were too badly damaged to sail for two months, Warren, now promoted Colonel, chartered for the task the large, heavily gunned privateers *Heureux* and *Prince Conti* at Saint-Malo.

Warren and his companions, who included Captain Sheridan the nephew of Sir Thomas, set sail on 20 August, 1746. On the morning of the 24th they had to take evasive action off Ushant when a British warship gave chase, but they managed to elude the enemy vessel. In variable winds for the next ten days the two ships made their way north round the west coast of Ireland. Many ships were sighted but none troubled them, and on the morning of 4 September the hills of Barra were visible on the horizon. They steered a course south of Barra Head, sailed up the east coast of Long Island, and entered Loch Boisdale in South Uist. Here the ships sent their boats ashore, and a party marched to Boisdale's home to seek information of the Prince's whereabouts, and to demand fresh provisions. The men found that Boisdale had been taken away prisoner, but met Rory Macdonald who had been one of the crew which rowed Flora Macdonald and the Prince to Skye. He advised them to leave Uist rapidly as the militia knew of their arrival and were assembling to attack them. He also offered to pilot them across the Minch to the mainland and set them on the tracks of the Prince who was hiding there.

Rory Macdonald took them over the channel and into Loch-nan-Uamh which they entered flying British colours to deceive any militia in the neighbourhood. The two privateers then lay at anchor for two weeks during which, according to the log of the *Prince Conti*, 'it blew a gale which kept other shipping away'. When the gale died out, the captains, anxious in case their ships should be caught at anchor by intruders as the *Mars* had been earlier, sailed out into the Minch to see that the coast was clear, and then returned. Meanwhile, Captain Sheridan had gone ashore and shown their credentials, and Major John Macdonald of Glenaladale, whom Sheridan contacted, had set off to find the Prince. Unfortunately Glenaladale thought the Prince was still near Achnacarry where he had met him while he was under the care of Cameron of

Clunes; and when he reached that area, not even Clunes's family knew exactly where he had gone. Glenaladale set about roaming Lochiel's devastated homeland and had just passed the burnt ruin of the chief's castle when quite by accident he encountered a woman who gave him the information he was seeking. She said the Prince had crossed the River Lochy and gone off to lodge in a hide-out in Badenoch. The search for him was now taken up first by the son of Cameron of Clunes and then by John McColvain, and Glenaladale returned to Loch-nan-Uamh to make certain the ships waited until he was found.

In his narrative of the events of those days, Cluny Macpherson states that McColvain would not have found the Prince but for a chance meeting in the darkness of the autumn night with Lochiel's brother and himself as they were going back to collect their share of the gold buried near Borrodale. As it was, however, Cluny sent back one of his followers with McColvain, and thus at last the news of the arrival of the ships in Loch-nan-Uamh reached the Prince in 'The Cage' high up on the slopes of Ben Alder.

Miniature of Charles by Jean-Louis Tocqué

L

Charles set out with those who were to accompany him to France: Colonel Roy Stewart, Chevalier Lancize, Dr. Cameron and Colonel Macdonell of Lochgarry, whose remnant of Highlanders – along with Macphersons – had been guarding the Prince in 'The Cage'. They moved slowly, taking every precaution to avoid being intercepted by the men of Lord Loudoun's regiment and General Campbell's militia who were in the neighbourhood. The crucial point was the crossing of the Lochy, for the militia had destroyed all the boats they could find on the river. Fortunately, they discovered a leaky old craft which got them safely across, and from the far bank they went on without mishap down to Loch-nan-Uamh.

According to an eye-witness, 'the ships sailed between two and three in the morning, with the wind very fresh at north'. They soon cleared the loch, and stood out for the open sea; and then the Prince went up on deck and took a last sad look at Scotland.

Appendix A

GENERAL WADE'S ROADS:
THE CLANS

Following the initial efforts at pacification in 1715, General Wade was given the task of bringing a degree of permanent law and order to the Highlands. At first he did not find his task easy, for he wrote in 1724, 'proper persons cannot be found to execute the offices of civil magistrates; especially in the shires of Ross and Inverness, and three deputy sheriffs are notorious Jacobites!' Wade's main achievements were the re-establishment of independent companies of Highlanders to act as police, and the building of more roads and bridges to make it easier for his armed forces to move about the country. There had been companies of Highlanders used as cattle-guards before, but these had been disbanded during the early Jacobite rebellions. In 1724 General Wade reconstituted six independent companies from clans loyal to the Government, not only to police the Highlands, but also to enforce the disarming acts. An attraction of the service was that the men of the independent companies were the only people allowed to carry arms. Three companies were composed of Campbells, and one each of Grants, Munroes and Frasers. They were provided with uniform, and their tartan of dark blue, black and green sett came to be recognized as the Government tartan. They were police, hence the word watch, and black in appearance compared with red-coated soldiers. Possibly they were also black because in the eyes of the Jacobites they were blacklegs. Although the name Black Watch was used from the start, it did not become the official designation until the nineteenth century, and in 1725 they were called Independent Highland Companies.[1] Wade also set about building roads and bridges. He used soldiers as roadmakers and paid them a bonus to encourage hard work. He also enlisted men for the job and gave them a distinctive uniform (a button from that of the Ross-shire company is shown on page 155). By 1737 the roads he planned had been completed, along with substantial inns at ten-mile intervals to replace the hovels there had been to accommodate travellers. One new highway linked Inverness with Fort Augustus and Fort William, passing along the

1. *Some were formed into a regular regiment in 1739 (43rd, later 42nd) and fought at Fontenoy in 1745.*

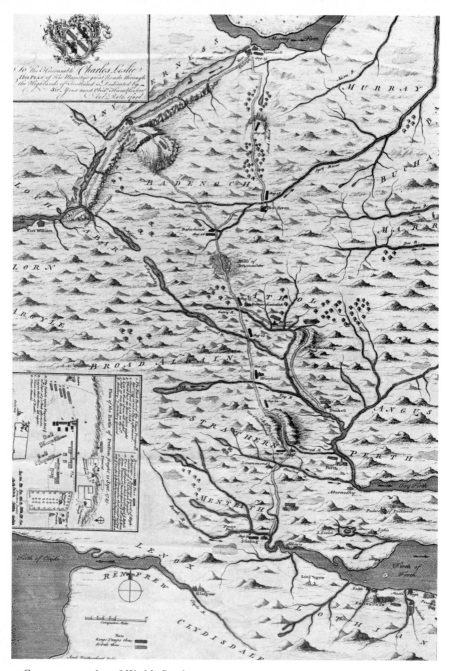

Contemporary plan of Wade's Roads

shores of Loch Ness; a reconstituted road led from the south of Loch Ness westwards past the 1719 battlefield at Glenshiel to Bernera barracks on the coast. The most difficult new road to construct began at Aberchalder and crossed the Monadhliath Mountains at the Corriearrack Pass, on the far side of which Wade had to construct a number of wide zig-zags to obviate a precipitous descent; this road continued to Dalwhinnie and Dalnacardoch, and one branch then ran past Blair to Dunkeld and another to Crieff and Stirling. Another important branch road went from Dalwhinnie past Ruthven barracks in Badenoch to the fort of Inverness. In this way all the main forts and barracks were linked with good roads.

The button worn by the Ross-shire company of Wade's road- and bridge-building soldiers

The total military strength of the Highland clans about this period (1737–1745) was estimated by those most competent to judge at twenty thousand men. Either Wade or Duncan Forbes of Culloden (it is not certain which) furnished the Government with a carefully compiled list of the clans and their fighting strength, entitled 'Memorial anent the true state of the Highlands as to their Chieftenries, Followings, and

Dependances before the late Rebellion' (i.e. 1745) of which the following is the concluding summary:[1]

Campbells	3000	**Mackgregors	500
**Mackleans	500	**Duke of Atholl (Murrays)	3000
**Macklachlens	200	**Farquharsons	500
**Stewart of Apin	300	**Duke of Gordon	300
*Mackdougalls	200	**Grants (Strathspey & Urquhart)	850
*McDonald of Slate	700		
**McDonald, Clanronald	700	**Mackintoshes	800
**McDonald, Glengary	500	**Mackphersons	300
**McDonald, Kepoch	150	**Frazers	700
**McDonald, Glencoe	150	**Glenmoriston (Grants)	100
**Camerons	800	**Chisholms	200
**Mackleods	700	*Mackenzies	2000
**Mackinnons	200	Monroes	300
**Duke of Perth (Drummonds)	300	Rosses	300
		Sutherland	700
**Robertsons	200	Mackays	500
**Menzieses	300	*Sincklairs	500
**Stewart, Garntilly	200		

1. *W. D. Norrie provides the information that the Jacobite clans are marked with an asterisk. Those that were out for Prince Charles in 1745 with two. In the case of some clans, such as the Macleans, Macleods, Gordons, and Grants, although the chiefs did not take the field, numbers of their clansmen fought on the Stuart side under cadets or lesser chieftains. The Murrays of Atholl were out with Duke William and Lord George Murray, and many of the Gordons under Lord Lewis Gordon.*

The following is a list of the officers of eighteen of the independent companies, being the whole number raised, with the dates of the delivery of their commissions on the completion of their companies, and of their arrival at Inverness:

	Captains	Lieutenants	Ensigns	Dates of completing the companies and of their arrival at Inverness
1	George Monro	Adam Gordon	Hugh Monro	1745 Oct. 23d
2	Alexander Gun	John Gordon	Kenneth Sutherland	25th
3	Patrick Grant	William Grant	James Grant	Nov. 3d
4	George Mackay	John Mackay	James Mackay	4th
5	Peter Sutherland	William Mackay	John Mackay	8th
6	John Macleod	Alexander Macleod	John Macaskill	15th
7	Normand Macleod of Waterstein	Donald Macleod	John Macleod	
8	Normand Macleod of Bernera	John Campbell	John Macleod	
9	Donald Macdonald	William Macleod	Donald Macleod	
10	William Mackintosh	Kenneth Mathison	William Baillie	18th
11	Hugh Macleod	George Monro	Roderick Macleod	28th
12	Alexander Mackenzie	John Mathison	Simon Murchison	Dec. 20th
13	Colin Mackenzie of Hilton	Alexander Campbell	John Macrae	
14	James Macdonald	Allan Macdonald	James Macdonald	31st
15	John Macdonald	Allan Macdonald	Donald Macdonald	
16	Hugh Mackay	John Mackay	Angus Mackay	1746 Jan. 6th
17	William Ross	Charles Ross	David Ross	8th
18	Colin Mackenzie	Donald Mackaulay	Kenneth Mackenzie	Feb. 2d

1 The Monros
2 and 5 The Earl of Sutherland's men
3 The Grants
4 and 16 The Mackays
6, 7, 8 and 9 The Macleods, under the laird of Macleod
10 A company raised in the town of Inverness
11 The Macleods of Assint, raised by Captain Macleod of Geanies
12 and 13 The Mackenzies of Kintail
14 and 15 The Macdonalds of Skye
17 The Rosses
18 The Mackenzies of Lewis

Culloden Papers History of the Highland Regiments, Highland Clans etc. (Keltie)

M

Appendix B
CHARM-STONES

Struan the chief of the Robertsons brought with him in 1745 the clan charm-stone, the *Clack-na-Bratach* or Stone of the Standard. This is said to have been acquired as early as 1315 when the Robertson chief of the time, while journeying with his clan to join Robert the Bruce's army before Bannockburn, saw on his standard, as it was being lifted one morning, a glittering object in a clod of earth clinging to its base. It was a ball of rock crystal about the size of an apple. He showed it to his followers and told them he felt sure that its brilliant lights were a good omen foretelling victory. And a victory was indeed won. From that time onwards whenever the clan was 'out' the *Clack-na-Bratach* was carried by the chief, and its varying hues indicated victory or defeat. When victory was likely it shone brightly whereas defeat was probable if it looked dark. On the eve of Sheriffmuir Struan Robertson consulted the stone and was horrified to observe a dark central patch as if formed by a large internal flaw. The Robertsons were not the only clan to carry charm-stones into battle, for at least three clans involved in the '45 possessed them. The Macdonells of Keppoch had one described as 'an oval of rock crystal about the size of a small egg fixed in a bird's claw of silver with a small chain attached by which it was suspended when about to be dipped'. A Gaelic incantation was repeated over the stone at the dipping ceremony, which was performed in water taken from St. Bridget's Well near Keppoch. The Stewarts of Ardsheal had a crystal sphere banded with silver with a chain attached. And the Stewarts' deadly rivals the Campbells had a crystal ball over five inches in diameter known as its Victory Stone or *Clack-Buaidh*.

BIBLIOGRAPHY

Albemarle Papers (ed.)   C. S. Terry 2 vols. (London 1902)

Allardyce, J. (ed.)   Historical Papers relating to the Jacobite Period 1699–1750 2 vols. (Aberdeen 1895–6)

Atholl Chronicles

Culloden Papers   1625–1748 ed. D. G. Forbes (1815)

Culloden Papers   (ed.) D. Warrand 5 vols. (London 1929–30)

Jacobite Relics   Scottish National Library

Kirkconnel Papers

Lockhart Papers   2 vols. (London 1817)

State Papers Scotland

Stuart Papers   ed. F. H. Blackburne Daniell. Historical Manuscripts Commission – Calendar of Stuart Papers, Windsor Castle 7 vols. (London 1902–23)

Stuart Papers at Windsor   ed. A. and H. Tayler (London 1939)

Vernon Papers   (ed.) B. McL. Ranft (Navy Records Society 1958)

Richard Warren Papers   Archive Départementale, Vannes, France

* * * *

Adam, Frank   The Clans, Septs and Regiments of the Scottish Highlands (Edinburgh and London 1970)

Blaikie, W. B.   Itinerary of Prince Charles Edward Stuart (Scottish History Society 1897)

Bolitho, Hector   The Galloping Third (London 1962)

Buchan, John   A History of the Royal Scots Fusiliers (London 1925)

Chambers, R.   History of the Rebellion of 1745–6 (London 1869)

Charles, G.   Transactions in Scotland during the years 1745–6 Vol. II

Charteris, E.   William Augustus, Duke of Cumberland (London 1913)

Cowper, L. I.   The King's Own (4th): The Story of a Royal Regiment (Oxford 1939)

Doddridge, P.   Some Remarkable Passages in the Life of Colonel James Gardiner (Edinburgh 1772)

Duke, Winifred   Prince Charles Edward and the Forty-Five (London 1938)

Elcho, D.	A Short Account of the Affairs in Scotland in the Years 1744–6 (London 1907)
Fergusson, James	Argyll in the Forty-Five (London 1951)
Forbes, Archibald	The Black Watch (London 1896)
Forbes, R.	(ed. Henry Paton) The Lyon in Mourning (London 1895)
Forbes, R.	(ed. Robert Chambers) Jacobite Memoirs of the Rebellion of 1745 (London 1834)
Fortescue, John	History of the British Army Vol. II (London 1899)
Gibson, J. S.	Ships of the '45 (London 1967)
Hamilton, H. B.	Historical Record of the 14th (King's) Hussars 1715–1900 (London 1901)
Home, John	The History of the Rebellion in Scotland (Edinburgh 1822)
Johnstone, Chevalier de	Memoirs of the Rebellion in 1745 and 1746 (London 1821)
Keltie, John S.	(ed.) A History of the Scottish Highlands, Highland Clans and Regiments (Edinburgh 1875)
Kingsford, C. L.	The Story of the Royal Warwickshire Regiment (6th Foot) (London 1921)
Lang, A.	Prince Charles Edward (London 1900)
Linklater, Eric	The Prince in the Heather (London 1965)
Murray, J.	(ed.) R. F. Bell. Memorials of John Murray of Broughton (London 1898)
Norrie, W. Drummond	The Life and Adventures of Prince Charles Edward Stuart 4 vols. (London 1900)
Prebble, John	Culloden (London 1961)
Ray, J.	A Compact History of the Rebellion (London 1748)
Rennie, J. A.	In the Steps of the Clansmen (London 1951)
Richmond, H. W.	The Navy in the War of 1739–48 (Cambridge 1920)
Salmond, J. B.	Wade in Scotland (Edinburgh 1938)
Scott, Sir Walter	The Tales of a Grandfather (London 1898)
Sinclair-Stevenson, Christopher	Inglorious Rebellion (London 1971)
Taylor, I. C.	Culloden – a Guide-book to the battlefield with the story of the battle (Edinburgh, National Trust)
Terry, C. Sandford	The Forty-Five, a narrative of the last Jacobite Rising by several contemporary hands (London 1901)

Tomasson, Katherine   The Jacobite General (London 1958)
Tullibardine, The   A Military History of Perthshire 1660–1902
Marchioness of (ed.)   (Glasgow and Edinburgh 1908)
Weaver, Lawrence   The Story of the Royal Scots (London 1915)

INDEX

LEWIS
STORNOWAY

THE MINCH

HARRIS

LONG ISLAND

NORTH UIST

BENBECULA

SKYE

SOUTH
UIST

SLEAT

BERNERA *Glensh*

BARRA

ERISKAY

BARRISDALE

KINLOCH

GLENFINNAN

Barra
Head

BORRODAL
Loch-nan-Uamh

Loch Shiel

KINLOCHMO'DART

INVERARA

■ Castles or homes of Chiefs

◗ Forts and barracks

——— PRINCE CHARLES

– – – GENERAL WADE